HOW TO RESTORE

Car Interiors

OSPREY
RESTORATION
GUIDE 2

HOW TO RESTORE
Car Interiors

Peter Wallage

First published in 1983 by Osprey Publishing Limited
59 Grosvenor Street, London W1X 9DA
First reprint autumn 1984
Second reprint summer 1985
Third reprint winter 1985
Fourth reprint spring 1986
Fifth reprint spring 1987
Sixth reprint autumn 1988

Sole distributors for the USA

Osceola, Wisconsin 54020, USA

British Library Cataloguing in Publication Data

Wallage, Peter
    Car interiors.—(Osprey restoration guides)
    1. Automobiles—Upholstery
    I. Title
    629.2′6   TL275
ISBN 0-85045-519-7

Editor Tim Parker
Associate Editor Graham Robson

Filmset and printed in England by
BAS Printers Limited, Over Wallop, Hampshire

Special thanks to John Charles of Barry Simpson Restoration, Newton
Abbot, and Richard and Trisha Pilkington of the Totnes Motor
Museum

CONTENTS

Chapter 1 | Taking things apart

Refurbishing the interior of a car—refurbishing as distinct from re-upholstering, which is dealt with in another book in this series—is one of the more rewarding projects in car restoration because, unlike most mechanical jobs, you see and appreciate the result of your efforts every time you use the car.

In many ways it is also easier than working on the mechanics or the bodywork because there no special tools are required, and very little in the way of technical knowledge or specialist training is needed. But, like most things, there is a right and a wrong way of going about the job.

Dispel once and for all the idea that you can come back from your local accessory shop armed with a few tins of wonder cleaner and, in a leisurely afternoon's work, make good the general wear and tear of years, some possibly including sad neglect. Tackling the job the wrong way leads to disappointment and excuses, if only to yourself, for the parts which 'didn't come up quite as they should have done'. Tackling it the correct way gives an interior you can be proud of. The aim of this book is to show you the correct way.

Before you start on the actual refurbishing, you will have to do some detective work to find out why, for example, the rear parcel shelf and the headlining round the rear window are badly stained, why the polish has disappeared from only *one* side of the wooden capping rail across the top of the dashboard or why the carpet on one side has gone quite rotten and the pile pulls away in your fingers.

Most of these ailments are caused by damp. Some of it may be due to condensation, but it is more likely to be because of leaks round the rubber window seals or even

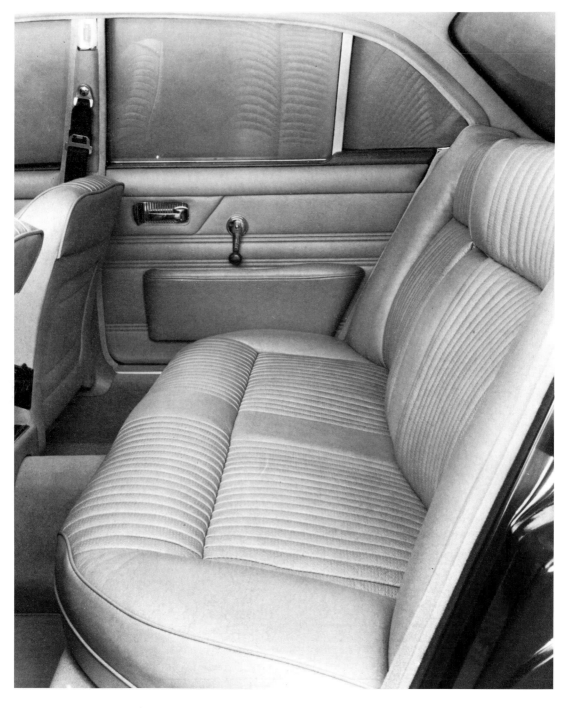

Left **More luxurious than some examples, but still quite easy to take out and replace though there may be hidden bolts or spring catches to puzzle you**

Right **Here we are seeing more complication on a Jaguar XJ-S, with a rear seat moulded to the car body. In a few cases like this there may even be screws inside the boot holding the backrest in place**

Below **A plain and simple rear seat—no trouble to lift out and no trouble to put back again. This car was photographed when new, by the way, and the fits were not perfect!**

through some of the spot welded seams in the wheel arches. Though putting these faults right comes more into the category of bodywork repair than interior refurbishing, they have to be put right before you tackle the interior or your work will be wasted.

Unless the rubber window surrounds have aged to the point where they are cracking, there are a number of preparations on the market which will make them watertight once again, and there are caulking and sealing compounds which can be used to reseal spot welded seams where the original sealing compound has dried out and cracked. If you find this somewhat specialized compound difficult to obtain, you can use one of the two-pack preparations more

If you decide to take the covering off the seats, you will find a number of fastenings, including metal clips and even wire

Left **Always number the back of each panel as you take it off**

Below **When you finally have it all stripped out, the interior is likely to look very sorry, and you might begin to wonder how it is all going to go back together! But if you have numbered each panel as it came off, you have no difficulties**

Right **The door trim panel of this
Austin-Healey 3000 is clearly held
in place to the door skins by a
series of small screws, which are
obvious. Once this, and the rest of
the 'furniture and fittings' is
removed, it should be easy to get
at the window winding
mechanism and locks, if needed**

Below **Restoring a relatively
modern car to this (new)
standard is a long and
complicated business. When
stripping out a scruffy example,
you should not only number or
mark everything, but take
reference pictures, and have
manufacturers' shots like this to
hand, for guidance**

Above **The clue to removing many a trim pad is not obvious without looking around their corners. On this Aston Martin DB5, the waist-level pad on the door is held in place by screws hidden when the door is closed**

Above **On a car like this Aston Martin DB5, the way to dismantle all the door trims, and details, is relatively obvious. First, remove the handle, near the hinge, then unscrew the trim panel from the door itself. This car, of course, has electric-winding window operation**

Below **A complex fascia—this is an Aston Martin DB5—should be studied carefully, and even photographed, before you start to strip it down for full renovation. The radio has already been taken out of the console**

Left **Many neglected classic cars have detail fittings missing, particularly if they have been stored, or 'cannibalized' over the years. This DB5, thank goodness, is still complete, except that the radio has temporarily been removed**

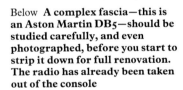

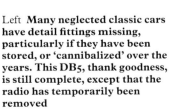

Right **The joy of a truly simple car! This is an Allard door—and the owner will never have difficulty in performing a strip down. More complex, more modern, saloons are rarely as easy as this**

Below **The screws all the way up the side of the Bentley door frame are to fix some items of trim to the door shell. It is little clues like this which will allow you to tackle a rebuild without having to resort to brute force, or break anything**

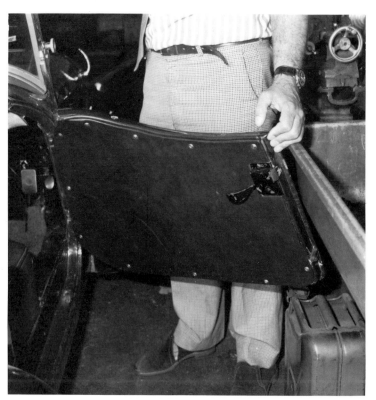

If there is no other visible means of removing a door trim panel, try levering it gently with a broad bladed screwdriver. It may be held by spring clips, but watch out for small screws through the edges of the door that are sometimes used with brackets to hold the trim

usually employed for filling dents in bodywork—such as David's Isopon or Plastic Padding.

Tackling these jobs will mean taking out the seats, the carpets and possibly some of the interior trim panels as well. They will have to be removed for a complete refurbishing in any case, and you may be surprised to see the large number of trim panels which are likely to accumulate round the car. Unless you are absolutely certain that you can remember where each one fits and the order in which you took them out, it is a sound plan to number each panel on the back and to keep notes of its location. It can be most annoying when you are replacing things, to find you have to take half the trim out again just to tuck the edge of one panel behind another.

Taking the carpets out may mean taking out the front seat runners as well, but the method of removal is usually self evident. Not quite so evident is the way some trim

Above **Some interior door furniture is held by a screw, but quite often it is held by a small pin under a spring loaded escutcheon**

Top **The method of taking out most seat runners is self evident, but on some, with semi-automatic positioning, unhook the spring before you loosen the bolts**

panels are held in place. They may be located by chromium plated screws and cup washers, but they are more likely to be held by hidden clip fasteners. If there is no obvious means of fastening the panel, try levering the edge up gently with a broad bladed screwdriver, then move it along until you come to a point where the panel is firmly held down. A little extra leverage will, in most cases, spring the clip out of its hole in the bodywork, but if this does not happen readily make sure there is no other form of fastening holding it in place—such as a screw through the side of a door pillar.

The interior door handle and the window winder will have to be removed before the door trim can be taken off, and there are a number of ways in which these are held. Some have a simple screw fixing, but a hidden pin is more likely, which is held in place by a spring loaded escutcheon plate under the handle or winder. The escutcheon plate has to be pushed back against its interior spring before this pin can be pushed out; though there are special tools available for doing this it can usually be accomplished by using two screwdrivers, one each side, to wedge the plate back while the pin is pushed out with either a thin parallel sided punch or a small instrument screwdriver. You may need help for this! Most of these pins are parallel, but a few are tapered, so if it does not tend to come out easily, try pushing it from the other direction.

In addition to the escutcheon plate and its spring, there may well be a number of other washers and distance pieces, so after removal thread them all in order on a piece of string to make matters less complicated when the time comes to put them back, and take care to preserve the small pin.

Keep all the parts of interior handle fittings in order and try not to lose the small pin!

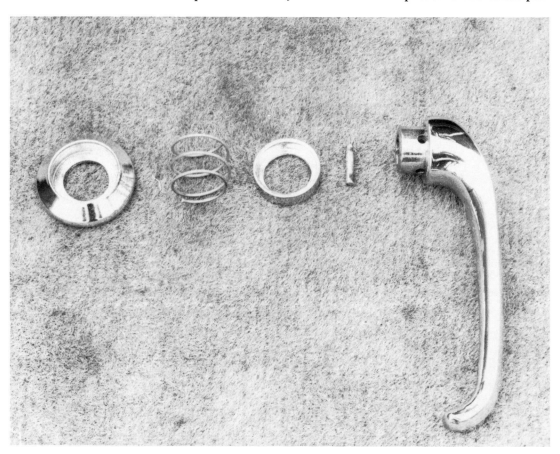

It is one of those silly little items which are fiddling to make and for which it is often difficult to find a replacement if lost.

The door trim itself is most likely to be held round its edges by hidden clips, but if the car has wooden or material-covered finishing plates just below the door windows, the top of the trim is most likely to be trapped under this plate. Once again, you will come across a variety of ways of holding the plate in place. In some cases it will be held by screws which can be seen after the door capping rail is taken off, but if there is no visible means of holding it, the fastening is quite likely to be by a slotted plate or plates on the back, the slots of which engage with dome headed studs or bolts on the door frame.

On some luxury models you have the added complication of power operated windows in the doors. Make sure you can trace the wiring before you start taking the trim out

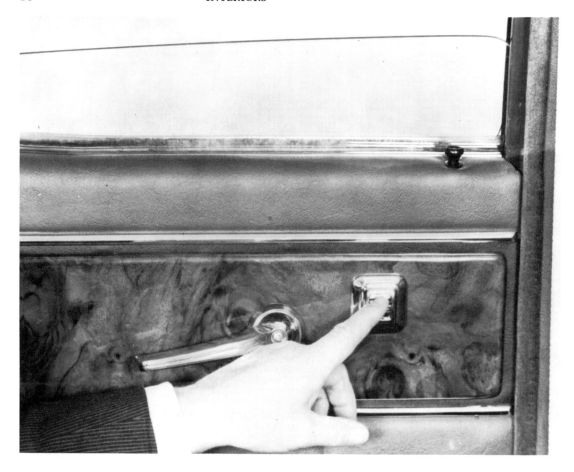

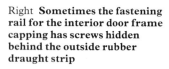

Above **Make sure you have disconnected the battery before you take off a door capping containing an electric window control switch**

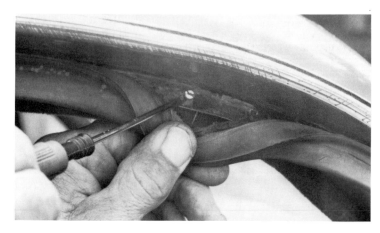

Right **Sometimes the fastening rail for the interior door frame capping has screws hidden behind the outside rubber draught strip**

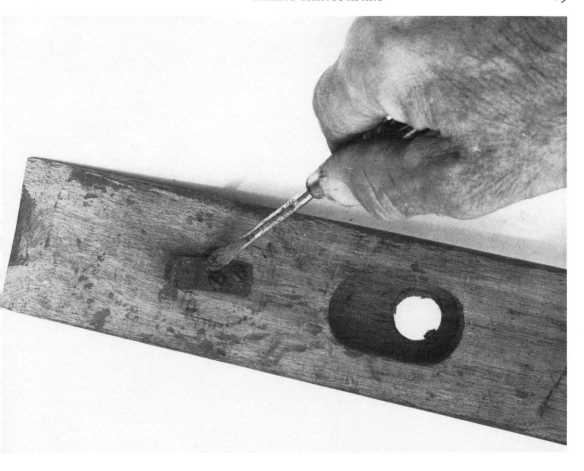

Some wooden trim panels are held by clips such as this and have to be pushed sideways to free them, but before you start thumping make sure there are no hidden screws

Try pushing it sideways before you start levering at it. In many cases you will find it tight, but thumping it sideways with the heel of one hand while you push it against the door with the other will usually shift it, *if* this is the method of fastening. In extreme cases you may have to tap it along with a padded block of wood and hammer, but take great care with wooden panels, because the edges of the fine veneer are very thin, and easily damaged.

The wooden capping rail over the top of the dash is usually held from underneath either by wood screws or by studs and nuts with, once again, a slotted plate fastened to the underside of the rail. If you find studs and nuts, loosen them and try sliding the capping rail backwards

A clue to the dismantling of this Humber fascia is the use of screws with chrome washers at various points. The under-fascia pads, too, are simply screwed up to the fascia structure

before you take the nuts completely off. The designer sometimes puts slots in the plates for the very good reason that though you may be able to reach the nuts with a socket on the end of a long extension bar to remove them, it is almost impossible to get a hand up to put them back on again, without taking out most of the rest of the dashboard and the instruments.

Talking about polished wood and dash panels leads me to mention the agonising decision you must make of

Three types of instrument cluster on a relatively modern car, each with its own problems for the restorer. In cases such as this, try to take the instrument panel out complete and dismantle it on the bench rather than strip it out while it is in the car

whether or not to take a polished wood dash out of the car to refurbish it, which means tackling the awkward and complicated business of disconnecting the instruments and wiring, or whether to try to do the job with the panel still fastened to the car and the instruments in place. I will deal with this problem more fully in the chapter on refinishing interior woodwork, but for the moment—unless you are very sure of your skills behind the dash—I would advise leaving it in place.

Unless you intend renewing all, or part, of the headlining I would advise that you leave this in place too. If it is a plastic material you can clean it quite easily in situ, and if it is a woolcloth it cannot be washed without shrinking. A badly stained woolcloth headlining, therefore should be renewed. Part repairs such as renewing the panel round the rear window—the rear curtain as it is sometimes termed—or repairing a small snag or tear can be done without taking the headlining right out, and once again I will deal with that in the appropriate chapter. The same applies to sunshine roofs.

Opposite **The centre console on this Jaguar E type is much less complex than it looks. The basis is simple metal foldings, and the trim panels can easily be renovated or replaced by the DIY restorer**

Below **The Rover (P 5) 3-litre dash and instruments looks complicated (and rather fussy) but it comes apart in sections which makes things easier for the restorer**

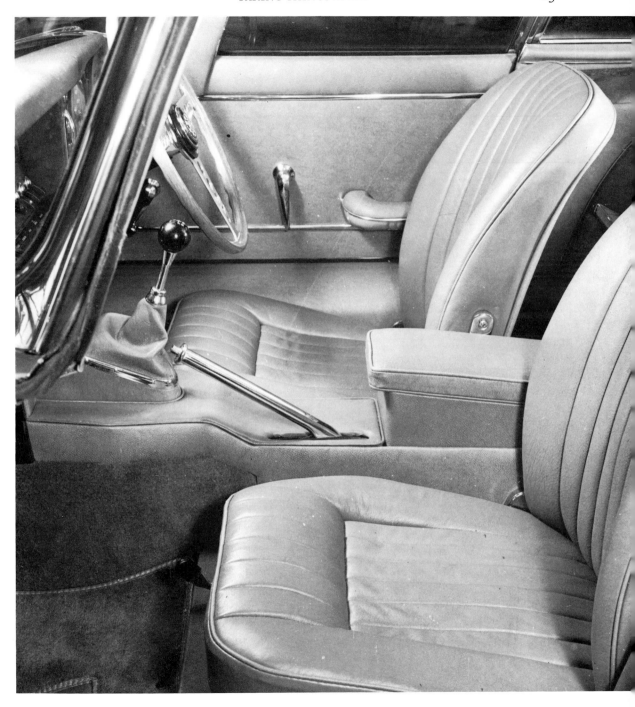

Don't be discouraged, for at this stage of strip down everything looks so run down. With patience, however, this Riley RM saloon will be restorable

Taking out the carpet and the interior trim panels will have revealed any rust which has been caused by leaks, so before you go any further with the refurbishing, wire brush any rusty patches, treat them with a rust killer and give a good coat of primer to the floor panels, the interior of the doors, and all the metalwork you have exposed by taking off the trim panels. Later, you may decide to coat these areas with a body sealing compound to give extra protection and to cut down panel drumming, but any worthwhile body sealing compound stays flexible instead of drying out, so this is one of the last jobs you should do before the carpeting and panels go back or you will get yourself and the panels into a dreadful mess. While you have all the interior out of the car you may also decide to make it quieter by incorporating some form of sound deadening material.

Chapter 2 | Cleaning the trim

Before you start the job of cleaning the seats or trim panels, tackle any small repairs which may be necessary. Pulling together seams where the stitching has started to come adrift can often be tackled quite successfully without dismantling the covering, by using a small curved needle. There is quite an art in this, not the least part of which is to push it through several layers of hide.

Experienced upholsterers use a 'palm', rather like a fingerless leather glove with a non-slip pad in the centre, but with a small curved needle I find this gets in the way. In extreme cases I have to take things slowly, the hard way, and use a pair of pliers rather than push the blunt end of the needle into my hand. Use button thread, and rub it across a block of beeswax both to preserve it and to make it easier to run through the hide.

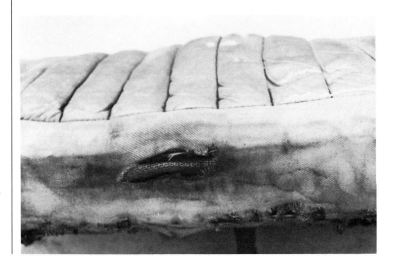

In some cases the makers of seats economized on hide by using cloth where it didn't show. There is no need to be too fussy, for a simple sewn-on patch will make an adequate repair

There are a number of special knots that upholsterers use to lock each stitch, but though these are most effective when working from the back of a hide, I find they tend to show when you are working on a repair of the panel from the front. The least 'visible' way I have found, is to tie a knot in the end of the thread in the usual way and bury this somewhere down in the trim vee where the seam is coming adrift so that it never shows. To fasten off a thread in the middle of a seam, go back through the previous stitch

Often you can repair a seat seam which is gaping by using a curved needle without taking the covering right off

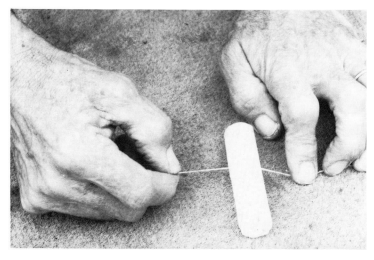

Before you use thread, rub it across a block of beeswax or even a candle to make it run through the material more easily

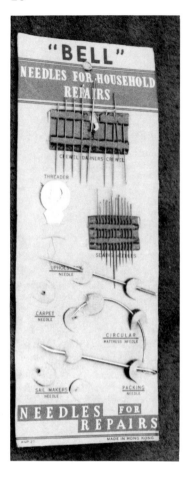

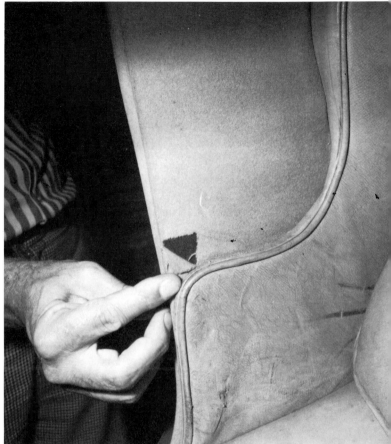

Above **A useful pack of needles for tackling upholstery and carpet repairs**

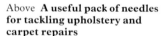

Right **This tiny triangular tear in the cloth trim near a door opening can be disguised, not only by chasing a similar patch inside the original material, but by carefully sticking down the torn piece again. Your patience could be rewarded—for it would be costly to replace the whole panel**

and form a slip knot, before pulling the thread tight.

Right-angled tears and slits in a panel present more of a problem. Invisible repair is not possible for any attempt at sewing them is bound to show. The only reasonably successful way I have found to repair these without renewing the whole panel is to get in behind them and stick on a patch. In a few cases it is possible to work a patch in from the outside of the panel, apply adhesive with a brush through the tear and press the torn edges down against the patch, but the results will always be obvious, whichever method is used.

The covering will probably be held to the seat, or squab frame, by a series of clips, and in addition it may be held

Above **Lush and luxurious looking—but the seat covers on the 1600E Cortina are moulded (even the 'stitches' are moulded) and if they become torn the only satisfactory solution is to replace**

Left **This sort of small tear is a nasty one to hide. The best way to repair is to stick a patch on the back and then treat the front with leather dye and lacquer**

Right **On the type of seat which has a foam interior, the covering is often stuck to the foam. It is almost impossible to get it off without destroying the foam**

with adhesive in some places. If it is firmly stuck, *don't* pull hard for even if you do not tear it you will certainly stretch it beyond recall. The original adhesive may not be the same as the one you use, but most have a similar base, and respond to the cleaner or thinners which you can buy for the new adhesive. This thinner or cleaner is a petroleum-based liquid, so keep it away from the finished side of the hide or vinyl, as it will certainly destroy the surface finish. Use a small paint brush of the type found in children's paint boxes, and use the minimum of thinners against the old adhesive to soften it.

I have never had much success with iron-on or self-adhesive ready-made patches, and do not recommend them for they have all come off in a few months. I use a piece of material of the same type as the upholstery, and reasonably generous in size, and stick it to the back with an impact adhesive. So far, the best I have found is Aerosol Auto Adhesive, made by the 3M Company. It is more expensive than many, but is good. Unless you absolutely soak the join afterwards it will remain firmly stuck through normal cleaning. This means that you can make the repair before you use the upholstery cleaner.

You will never be able to make a tear completely invisible, but with colouring and lacquering applied after-

Left **Some panels, and even seats, have the pattern moulded into the vinyl. A sewn in patch always looks odd so it is best to look for seats in better condition if yours are damaged**

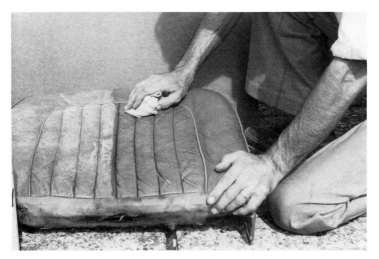

Left **The first stage in attending to the seats is to give them a thorough clean**

Below **Open sports cars such as this US specification Jaguar E type often suffer from exposure to the elements, and replacing the moulded trim can cost much more than you think. Careful refurbishing will often pay dividends**

This Aston Martin front seat is leather covered, but is showing signs of age and regular use. Nevertheless, you will certainly be able to clean it up still further, and restore the colour to its former glory, if you follow the procedures listed in these pages

wards, it is unlikely that it will be noticed except, perhaps, by a concours judge.

The cleaning compound you use on the seats and trim panels will be governed by the material with which they are upholstered. You will find plenty of brands of upholstery cleaner in your local accessory shop. While any reputable brand is quite safe to use on vinyl, some experts—among them Connolly Brothers which has sup-

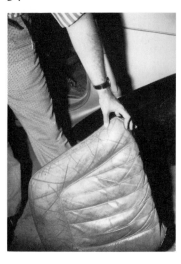

Left **Still comfortable, but badly creased, and badly stained—a leather seat cushion needing all the attention that someone like Connolly Bros can give it**

Right **A simple and uncomplicated interior needs careful refurbishing if it is to look well, particularly if it was cheap and cheerful in the beginning. There is nothing but the standard finish to set it off**

Below **Brushed nylon will wash, but brush the pile in the direction of its natural flow before it dries or it will look matted**

Year after year of bad weather, beating down on the tonneau cover of this sports car, have resulted in the front section becoming very stained. Patience—and diligence—will often allow you to smarten up the cover quite considerably

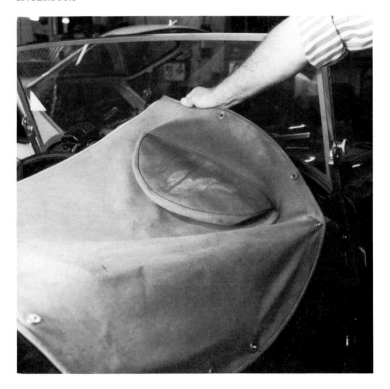

plied nearly all the hides used in British car upholstery almost since the dawn of motoring—are wary about recommending their indiscriminate use on leather hide.

Vinyl is impervious to water, but hide is not, and when water soaks into the hide any detergents which may be in the upholstery cleaner are carried with it. I have never had any problems with my own cars, but I am prepared to believe Connolly's experts when they say that, should you want to re-colour the hide there is a chance that some detergents may leach out again and produce a patchy result. They say that on hide you should use only a pure mild soap, not a coarse industrial soap which may still contain traces of the caustic material used in its preparation, and certainly not a household detergent, which probably contains a whitener, brightener, softener or some other product of modern industrial chemical technology.

I would advise against consulting a saddlery or similar shop (which caters for leather saddles and harness) for any

Naturally the seat covers of the Bentley R type, which is almost identical in this area with the Rolls-Royce Silver Dawn, are of real leather, and it is always worth treating them to a comprehensive valeting process when a rebuild is in progress. Messrs Connolly specialize in renovations of this type

leather cleaning and care preparations. Saddle soap, one of the standard preparations you will be offered in such shops, is excellent for equestrian leather, but is far too coarse for your purposes. It is intended for burnished leather. The hide used in car upholstery is lacquered and hot rolled, which is a very different process. You should also avoid Neat's Foot oil, obtained from cattle hooves, which is the standard preparation for softening and pre-

serving riding boots and harness leathers. This can stain car upholstery hides quite irretrievably.

On moquette, Bedford cord and any other cloth upholstery which is not a man-made fibre the use of detergent washing powders is a controversial point. Once again, the experts say you should use only a mild soap, but I have cleaned Bedford cord successfully with ordinary household washing powder detergent which lifted out many of the stains that plain soap had failed to shift. I have also used carbon tetrachloride with success on some of the more stubborn grease spots, but if you decide to use this, remember that it has very nasty fumes which attack the membranes at the back of your nose and throat. Should you smoke in the presence of these fumes you can do yourself a great deal of damage as they can generate a poisonous gas (I believe it is phosgene) when inhaled through a burning cigarette or pipe. The more vicious and even nastier industrial degreasing fluids such as trichloroethylene should all be avoided.

Whether you use a branded upholstery cleaner, a detergent washing powder or a pure soap, remember that it is the foam, and not the water which does the cleaning. Use a fairly soft brush such as a paint brush or soft shoe clean-

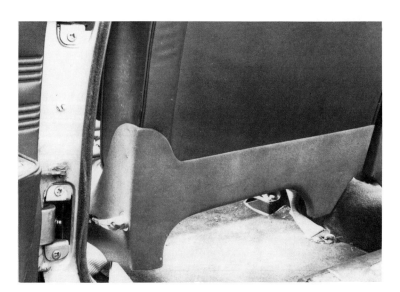

Many seats on luxury cars of the 1960s had a carpet covered base, but this had a much finer pile than the floor carpet

ing brush, *not* a scrubbing brush, and work up the foam to a good lather. Wipe this off with a cloth wrung out in clean water, and continue wiping until all the foam is lifted off. Doing this several times will make the upholstery even cleaner, and it will be less likely to leave it patchy than if you try to do the job in one fell swoop by soaking the upholstery in water.

Plastic headlinings which are undamaged will respond to the same cleaner treatment that you used on the vinyl seats; as I have already said you should repair any small tears or snags before you start cleaning.

Getting behind the headlining to put on a patch can sometimes be a problem because there are many different

Cord finish upholstery often cleans up surprisingly well with detergents, and if it is stained it can sometimes be dyed a darker shade to hide the stains. Use ordinary household cloth dye, diluted and sponged on in several applications

This R type Bentley has aged gracefully, but is still grubby, nevertheless, around the rear quarters. Identify the materials, and the best type of cleaning method, before ever applying lotion, cloth, or brush

ways of fixing the lining in place. For ease of production on many relatively modern cars the lining, complete with the steel roof sticks which hold it up, is sprung into place sometimes with a wire running round the outside which sits down in a groove in the bodywork. On others there is no stiff wire round the edges but there is sometimes a flexible wire cable which runs along the sides of the head-lining and which is anchored at the front and back. At the back it is usually anchored to a large self-tapping screw somewhere down by the parcels shelf and at the front quite a common practice is for the end of the flexible wire to run down the windscreen pillar, to be fixed to a nut and bolt (or stud and nut) underneath the dash somewhere so that the edges of the headlining can be made taut by pulling on the wire before the nut is tightened.

Sometimes the ends of this wire can be quite difficult to reach because on some production lines the headlining is put into the car before the shelf under the dash and even before many of the instruments and some of the wiring is inserted. Be prepared to hunt around under the dash before you can assume that the edge wire for the lining is a rigid one sprung into place and not a flexible one which has been tensioned.

On some other cars the edges of the headlining are merely fixed to the steel bodywork with adhesive, and you will have to lift this before you can get behind it. Sometimes condensation has weakened this adhesive over the years and it will yield to a blunt knife blade slid under the lining, but in other cases it holds together particularly hard and you may have to use some adhesive thinners on a small paint brush to free it. Once again, be very careful not to get any thinners on the outside surface of the plastic headlining.

The older type of woolcloth headlining presents more of a problem. In most cases it will need cleaning to bring it back to its as-new condition, but cleaning it without taking it out of the car is awkward, because it is difficult to rinse the foam from it. Taking it out and washing it often means that it shrinks, so that you then have difficulty in getting it back into place. If you are prepared to risk having to make a new headlining, after trying to clean a patchy one with foam it is worth a gamble, but if the lining is just darkened or faded to a uniform colour, a good brushing is probably the best alternative.

If you intend to try to clean a woolcloth headlining while it is still in the car you will have to strike a balance between getting it very wet—too wet—and getting it sufficiently wet to rinse the dirt out once the foam has loosened it. The headlining will probably stretch as you make it wet and if you then push too hard with the sponge or soft brush you will rub the topside of the headlining against the roof of the car. This, by itself, will do it no harm, but the

chances are that there is powdery surface rust on the
underside of the metal roof, this will then be picked up
by the wet headlining and will work its way through, eventually to dry out and stain the lining. It is really a matter
for you to decide, always bearing in mind that you must
be prepared to renew the lining should you make it worse
than it was before you started.

Ideally the headlining should be taut and free from
wrinkles, but most older woolcloth headlinings tend to sag
with age. An old car trimmer's tip to tighten up the headlining is to steam it. You can usually find a place in the
headlining, possibly where the interior light fits, at which
you can poke a rubber or plastic tube through. If you connect the other end of the tube to the spout of an electric
kettle, and play steam round the inside of the lining, it will
at first seem to sag even more but when it dries out it will
be much more taut than before.

To clean carpets use ordinary household carpet sham-
poo, after giving them a good beating, and clean with a
vacuum cleaner. Some parts of the carpeting, possibly
along the sills or the front edge of the rear seat support,
will be fixed to the bodywork by adhesive; it is easier to
clean these in place than to pull them away from the
bodywork unless, of course you need to take them out to
repair any metalwork underneath.

By this stage the inside of the car will be looking quite
bare, and you will have plenty of space to move round and
clean all the other bits and pieces, such as the dashboard,
the wood or metal trim finishers, the handbrake, steering
wheel and column. Probably the best thing to do at this
point is to give everything a good clean before you start
any restoration. For lifting the dirt I have found that a cloth
dipped in warm water with a splash of ordinary liquid household floor cleaner, then wrung out well, is as effective as
anything. Follow it up by using a cloth wrung out in clean
water, which makes it unlikely that you will leave any detergent behind to affect any restoration you want to carry
out.

With everything clean and revealing its wear and tear,
you are now in the more interesting position of beginning
the refurbishing and putting it all back into place.

Chapter 3 | Painted metal finishes

Refinishing the metal interior parts of the car (the dash, windscreen pillars, door finishers and other details) that are sprayed in the same colour as the body exterior is a straight forward enough job, but one which needs quite a lot of preparation. It can be extremely tricky and fiddling if you are aiming for a top quality result. There should be no half measures about it. Either you must rub down and respray all the interior metalwork or you must leave

Even expensive cars of the 1950s sometimes had very simple dashboard layouts with very complex instrumentation. This was an AC Aceca-Bristol after many years of use

it alone. The chances of being able to blend in one part of it exactly to match the colour of the rest of it are quite small.

As with the outside of a car, all the interior metalwork which you intend to paint has to be rubbed down, and any rust spots treated with a rust killer, before you go any further. Use a fine grade of 'wet and dry' rubbing down paper, but always use it wet. If you use a coarse grade you will leave scratches. As the interior paintwork of the car takes nothing like the hard wear of the outside, you will not need to build up a new surface with half a dozen coats of paint which, with rubbing down in between coats, would hide fine scratches.

Your main trouble is going to come from the things that get in the way and which have to be taken off before you can start work on the metalwork itself. Unless you intend

The lines of this Triumph Spitfire dash layout depend on a perfectly smooth paint finish for their effect. If such a layout is scruffy, it really ought to be stripped back to the bare metal and resprayed

Left If you find this sort of rust under the seats or the carpets, you must scrape it out and treat the metal before you go any further

Below If the black crackle of this MGB fascia panel has been damaged, you are in trouble, for touching up may be difficult if a true match is to be achieved, and—by definition—you can't smooth it all down and start again

Attend to any rust spots on the interior metalwork around the windows by using a rust killer, or it will soon break through the new paint

to renew the windscreen and rear window, or their rubber mouldings, it is an awful lot of trouble to take them out to respray the surrounding metal, for it is also possible that you will break the screen. Masking off the main part of the glass isn't the difficult bit. The difficulty comes in masking the rubber moulding so that you do not get a build up of paint against the masking tape, which always shows when you take it off.

Some people lift the edges of the moulding and push masking tape underneath it and then fold the tape over the rubber, but this often causes problems when you take it off because the tape may stick to the underside of the rubber and you often mess up the paintwork getting it off. An easier way is to cut ordinary notepaper into strips, about an inch to an inch and a half wide, push these under the edge of the rubber moulding, fold them back and fix them on the moulding or the glass with masking tape. When you take them out they will slide out from under the moulding quite easily.

Another awkward part to mask off properly is the draught stripping which runs round the door apertures. If you intend to renew it in the restoration it is best to take it off before you spray the metalwork. If you want to leave it in place make sure it is masked properly. Some of these

On the MGA in the late 1950s, the fascia layout was simple enough, but previous owners may have added extra instruments or switches, and possibly left the panel in a mess. At least the trimmed panel is flat, and with patience you could certainly restore it to as-new level

draught strips are finished in a pile material, usually a felt flock, and if you stick masking tape directly to it you will mess up the pile and never get it looking nice again. Use the same writing paper technique already described for the rubber mouldings providing you can manage to slot the paper behind the draught strip. However some of them are fixed quite closely to the metal and in that case all you can do is to mask off as carefully as possible and take great care when you are spraying that the masking is pushed well down into place.

You will never get proper access to a metal dash to spray it with the steering wheel in place, so this must be removed.

**Some steering wheels are
awkward to remove but many
have a simple nut under the horn
push. You need to take the wheel
off to get at the dash properly**

This in itself can be quite a traumatic experience, for in some cars the method of holding the wheel is far from obvious. You should consult a workshop manual or a knowledgeable member of the appropriate one-make club on how to remove the wheel.

Instruments, knobs and switches are an absolute curse, when you are spraying a metal dash. Ideally, they should all be taken out so that the dash is left completely bare. There is no doubt that if you are willing to undo all the wiring and cables this is the best method. Although you might be confident that you can remember how, and where, all the instrument connections are fixed my bet is that in a matter of days you will forget some of them, so label the end of each wire as you unfasten it and draw a diagram of the back of the instrument with the connection points similarly marked.

There are several methods of holding the instruments in place. The older circular dials are usually held in place by a metal strap and two knurled nuts, but some of the combined instruments are fixed in a panel and you must take off the front covering of the dash before the panel can be released. Sometimes this can be a particularly awkward job, but fortunately many of these combined instruments, particularly those with a ribbon-type speedometer, with the ammeter, oil pressure gauge, water temperature gauge and other indicators all built into one panel, are recessed behind the dash. If you slacken off the fixing screws slightly, you can often tuck some writing paper behind the panel but in front of the glass to mask them off. This means that you do not have to take them out completely.

Circular instruments with a chromium plated bezel are more awkward, for masking them off while they are fixed securely to the panel is seldom completely successful. Either there will be a ridge of paint at the edge of the masking which shows when you take the masking off, or you find that there is a fine line round the bezel of the instrument where the new paint hasn't adhered. If you don't want to take the instruments out completely, it is sometimes possible to slacken the fixing hoop at the back, push the instrument slightly forward through the dash and take off the bezel. The bezel usually comes off when you give it a quarter turn, rather like unscrewing the top of a pickle jar.

With the bezel off push a plastic bag round the instrument and—if it will go backwards through the dash—push it back slightly to leave the metal free. Alternatively, leave the bezel on, pull the instrument slightly forward, wrap it in a plastic bag and spray carefully round it so that the paint goes completely to the edge of the hole in the metal.

Many instruments from the 1950s and 1960s are held to the back of the dash by simple clamps like this or by a horseshoe clamp

To save disconnecting multiple
instruments you can sometimes
pull them forward once the
speedo cable is disconnected and
protect them with a plastic bag.
This is an Austin A30

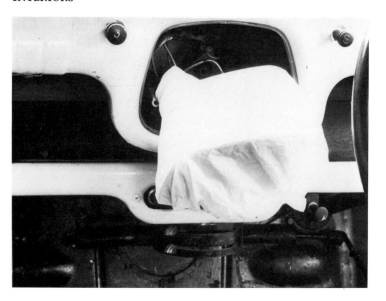

This is not the ideal solution, but on cars with complicated
wiring it is often an easy way out.

Many switches are fitted with a knurled chromium
plated fixing on the outside of the dash. These are quite
easy to slacken off and push through to leave the hole in
the dash clear, but on some cars the round knob of the
switch is too large to go through the hole and has to be
removed. Sometimes it can be unscrewed from the stem
of the switch, but on others there is a spring plate holding
it which can be released by pushing a small bradawl or tiny
screwdriver through a hole in the shank of the knob. The
hole is always on the underside of the knob—as you see
it—and is sometimes quite small, so it is easy to miss. On
some high grade cars the hole has been filled with a
coloured wax.

With all the fiddling bits of masking completed you must
then mask off the whole of the rest of the inside of the car.
Usually the steering column can be masked quite successfully with a plastic bag, but the headlining (if it is still in
place) will have to be masked carefully with sheets of
paper—old newspaper is very good for this—and masking
tape at the edges. Carry the masking over the whole of the
interior of the car. You may think, if you are only respray-

ing the front, that the rear part can be left unmasked, but in a confined space like the interior of a car, even with the doors opened, the spray will travel a surprising distance. To be on the safe side mask off *everything* which you do not want to be painted.

Any patches of bare metal which the rubbing down process has disclosed should be treated with a primer, then rubbed down again before you start to apply the undercoat and top coatings. Even if you have not uncovered any bare metal, it is always advisable to apply an undercoat before putting on the gloss finish. Most gloss finishes are slightly translucent, and need the solid body of the undercoat to give them a good depth of colour. Unless you are using a separate spray gun, one of the difficulties is going to be finding an undercoat in an aerosol can. If you cannot find one, a good alternative is to use one of the small portable aerosol sprayers where you have to fill a container with paint and then screw on a container of propellant, so that it works in much the same way as a spraygun and an airline. A modeller's air brush which can be bought quite cheaply in most model shops is even better. This will give you a fine spray and a degree of control which you can never achieve with the much coarser nozzle of the aerosol can. Air brushes can be used with a small compressor, but this is rather expensive, or with small cans of gas propellant which is cheaper for small jobs but more expensive if you are doing a lot of work.

Chapter 4 | Artificial wood graining

One of the most awkward and frustrating interior metal finishes to restore or reproduce is a wood grain effect. Many manufacturers used this kind of finish in the 1930s, and some carried on with it on their post-war models, until the vinyl-covered dash, usually with some form of anti-injury padding underneath it, took over. Originally, the grain patterns were screen-printed onto the sheets of flat metal before they were stamped out to shape, but towards the end of the 1930s the 3M Company produced a plastic film with a grain pattern on it called Di-Noc. Until recently, this material was still available to restorers, but towards the end of 1982, with demand practically gone from the automobile industry, and very little demand remaining from the makers of other appliances where wood grained plastic panels had taken over, the company discontinued it. Now, I understand, there is no stock left. You must therefore consider alternative action.

To produce a grained finish by hand requires a great deal of skill, and is something of an art. As with most arts, if you develop a flair you can excel and if not, the knack will rarely come with practice. I must admit right from the start that I am not very competent in producing grained finishes but I have seen experts in action and can describe the methods used and pass on their tips.

It is impossible to produce, by hand, an exact replica of the photo screen printed grain pattern that was used when the car was new, but unless a previous hand has already painted it over, it is worth taking a photograph of it so that, at least, you have an idea of which way the grain ran on the various pieces, and you have a reasonable chance of producing something similar.

The grain of the wood here looks a little too natural to be entirely true. Make certain every time you are dealing with real wood and not a photo-printed pattern before you start to apply paint stripper

To start the graining reproduction process the metal must be absolutely smooth and free from flaws even if this means flatting it back down to base metal. In many cases this will not be necessary; if the finish is rubbed down with wet and dry paper the old screen printed processes which were printed straight onto the metal will be suitable for graining again. If, however, the dash was covered with Di-Noc then the chances of producing a smooth finish without cutting through it are reduced. If you can achieve this without damage, then you can try to grain straight on top of the Di-Noc, but be warned that as Di-Noc is a plastic it is affected by some paints. Be prepared for it to go soft and curdle.

Whether you have flatted back to bare metal, or whether you try to get a new grain finish on top of the old plastic film, you must start off by applying a coat of primer. Use rubbing-down paper lightly, until the primer is perfectly smooth, with a satin finish. Now is the time to choose the base colour. In the past this varied from pattern to pattern but was usually some sort of blend ranging from a murky yellow to a fairly deep orange brown. This should be sprayed all over the metal and, when it has dried, very lightly rubbed down with wet and dry paper—sufficiently to take off any roughness and dust, but not enough to make it dead smooth, or the graining paint may not 'take' easily.

For putting on the design of the grain, different people like to use different materials. Some like to use an acrylic or enamel paint, some choose a water-based colour, and some people prefer to use a dark brown, or even black, printer's ink suitably thinned down.

The basic idea is that a coating of the graining paint must be laid over the base colour and then various implements are used to produce the grained patterned finish. It is possible to buy a graining tool in some art and craft shops. This usually looks rather like a quarter of a cylinder faced with hard rubber into which a series of lines are engraved. To produce the grained pattern, this is drawn along the work, while at the same time it is rocked. This works reasonably well on flat surfaces, but because it is an unyielding tool it is particularly awkward to use on curves, and almost impossible to use on re-entrant curves. Most professional graziers use a variety of tools to produce the pattern, ranging from old brushes and sponges, to screwed up pieces of newspaper. I have even read of a Californian graining expert who produces beautiful burr walnut graining by blowing on the wet graining coat through a drinking straw! Why not develop your own techniques on a spare piece of metal?

The grainer's brush is similar to an ordinary paint brush of about two inches width but with very much shorter and stiffer bristles. The ends of the bristles are sometimes notched and finished in an uneven edge. The grainer I watched working, used to make his own special brushes by cutting down an ordinary paint brush, and then cutting the end with a razor blade or scissors to produce an uneven edge. The sponge which he used was an ordinary slab of plastic foam, and he also used a grainer's comb which looks very much like an ordinary comb, except that it is made of hard rubber and the teeth are spaced more widely apart. The nearest approximation I have seen to this, outside of a craft shop, was a hard rubber comb intended for combing long haired dogs (which I found in a pet shop) or a rubber-bristled brush for using on suede shoes.

To produce the effect of knots in the wood is quite an art in itself. I watched it being done as follows: the grainer thumbed round with the corner of a sponge to produce the circular markings of the knot in several places across the metal panel. He then drew the graining brush along in long continuous sweeps from one side of the panel to the other waving it as he went along then sweeping in a swerve round the knot. This left the surface looking more or less grained but the bristles of the brush had left the effect rather too finely patterned. He followed this up with the comb, and in some cases with a corner of the sponge or a screwed-up piece of newspaper, again using continuous sweeps across the panel, waving his wrist as he drew the tool along.

His only method of describing what he did was to say: 'I just do what I think of at the time I am doing it, and if I don't like it I wipe the graining colour off, then try again until I get it looking right.'

My suggestion is that you obtain some old panels, coat them with base coat, choose a graining colour and practice for hours, either until you give up in disgust, and decide to paint the metalwork a plain base colour anyway, or you achieve sufficient expertise to be able to tackle the dash and window finishers themselves. There is one saving grace, which is that should you make a complete mess of the job you can always clean it off and start again.

Whatever type of paint you choose for graining, it will soon rub off again unless it is coated with a clear varnish. It does not matter very much which type of varnish is used except that it must be sprayed on. Any attempt at brushing on a varnish is likely to make the graining paint run, and produce fuzzy edges to the pattern. You must be very careful on one point, which is that you must choose a clear varnish, which will not react either with the base colour or the graining colour. Once again, a trial on a spare panel is recommended.

For most base and graining colours this rules out the use of a clear cellulose finish, but a clear acrylic enamel will 'take' successfully to most other paints, provided they have been allowed to dry first. Although I have never tried it, I am told that acrylic will 'take' equally well over the top of printer's ink, even though this never dries completely on metal. Therefore if you are using a printer's ink to produce the grained pattern, keep your fingers, and anything else well away from it until the coat of clear varnish has been sprayed on.

As an alternative to using the now non-existent Di-Noc, you could experiment with one of the other self-adhesive plastic films which can now be bought in most DIY shops; I knew of one restorer who successfully used the very thin plastic wood-grained film from the sheets of wall cladding which can be found in the same type of shop. He released it from the hardboard backing by playing a steam jet onto it and rolling the film round a broom handle. I have tried to do this myself, but every time I managed to start the lifting process, it tore. I never succeeded to getting a piece large enough to cover more than a glove box lid, but I suppose, as ever, there is a knack to this method.

Even when you have found a suitable wood-grained plastic film, you are still left with the problem of fitting it closely and snugly to the curved contours of the metal. If there is the slightest wrinkle or crease in the film, it looks absolutely awful. Fortunately most modern plastic films go quite soft and pliable when they are warmed, and if you warm the back of the panel in front of a low power electric fire or use an infra red heating lamp, the plastic can usually be persuaded to follow the contours reasonably successfully. Again, you should try to learn by your experience; the accepted technique is to start somewhere near the middle of the panel on a reasonably flat portion, then to work the plastic towards the edges with a cloth or your (clean) fingers, gently warming the back of the panel when it approaches any contour where it might not want to lie flat.

Most of the available self-adhesive wood grained plastic sheeting has nothing like the beauty of the pattern of the old Di-Noc (though some patterns are better than others), and though modern sheeting is very much cheaper in price, the quality is nothing like as good. So that they can stand up to any sort of wear, particularly around switches and knobs where they are likely to be rubbed by fingers, it is again essential for you to spray on a coat of clear protective varnish.

Chapter 5 | Repairing and revarnishing wood trim

To restore real wood trim strips and dashboards is very different from trying to imitate a photo-printed grain pattern, and—thank goodness—considerably easier. Most original finishes deteriorate, due to the effects of sunlight and condensation, and in some cases they tend to develop white streaky patterns, where the grain filler, which was inserted to fill the pores of the wood, has bleached back to its natural colour. Decide whether you will go the whole hog, and refinish all the interior woodwork in the car, or whether you will merely clean it, and wax it, to retain the slightly weathered look which some people associate with the older vehicles. But, as with painting the metal work in the interior, if you do only part of the job you will never

MG TAs and TCs looked like this. It was real wood for the fascia, but not of very high quality. Don't make the mistake of over-restoring when rebuilding such a car

Always resist the temptation to over-restore a car's interior. The instrument panel of this Allard was never more than neat and serviceable, so Rolls-Royce standards of veneer and polish would be quite inappropriate

The dash of this Austin does not look very complicated, but a surprising number of parts have to come off before you can take the wood out to strip and repolish it

**On a wooden instrument panel
you may find it easier to
disconnect the instruments and
take them out with the panel
rather than undo them with the
panel still in place**

match the colour completely, and the two different colours
will offend your eye every time you get into the car.

Ideally, you should take all the woodwork out of the car
before starting to refinish it. Where there are instruments
mounted through the wood you have to face the complication of all the wires and pipes that go to the back of them.
While it is possible to strip and refinish a dashboard by
easing the instruments slightly forward so that you can get
access to the edges of the holes, this is a very fiddling business and there is the real danger that a paint stripper used
to take off the old varnish will drop some spots on to the
instruments and the wiring, and possibly set up a lot of
future trouble. If you decide to do the work with the instruments still hanging on their wires and pipes, I would advise
covering each instrument with a plastic bag and taking this
back as far through the dash as possible to protect everything from the paint stripper.

For stripping off old varnish choose a paint stripper which does not affect the colour of the wood. This one can be neutralised with plain water

To use paint stripper is the only practical method of removing the old varnish. Many of the panels will be covered with veneer, and this is almost literally paper thin. If you try to remove the old varnish dry with a scraper there is an excellent chance that you will cut straight through the veneer. Almost any paint stripper will remove the old varnish successfully, but be wary of the very powerful ones which might contain the chemical called lye. While this is an excellent paint softener and stripper, it also has the unfortunate property of turning some types of mahogany and walnut a deep purple in the grain, and this purple colour is almost impossible to remove. I have had no such troubles with Polystrippa, which has another advantage, that it can be rinsed off with water. No doubt there are many other brands of stripper which will do an excellent job without staining the wood, but having found one which works well for me, I recommend it. I have always been a little wary of other paint strippers which need to be neutralized with white spirit or methylated spirit, because the only time I had the misfortune to inflict the purple colour on mahogany it was with one such stripper.

Before starting to put any stripper on the interior polished woodwork on your car, make absolutely certain that you *are* dealing with polished wood. Around the 1950s one or two manufacturers used wood for the main part of the interior finishing, but used a Bakelite type of plastic with a photo-printed wood grain in one or two places, such as the lid of the glove box. In case you think this practice

True quality, shown in the dignified instrument layout of a 1953 Bentley R type. You'd not be content with restoring a bad car to anything less satisfactory, would you?

was confined to cheaper cars, I should state that it was used on Bentleys and, as far as I know, on the Rolls Royce Silver Dawn as well.

Provided you have been dealing with real wood, the stripping of the old varnish will have left the surface slightly rough, where the liquids have raised the grain, and possibly there will be open pores in the grain, where the stripper has lifted out the grain filler. This is a type of coloured plaster mixture which is rubbed into the wood across the grain to fill up the open pores, and save on the amount of varnish needed to produce the smooth surface, as well as to save time with the varnishing coats. It is a production method of saving time which I would not recommend to you, because no home restorer counts his time; if you use successive coats of varnish to fill the grain, you will never suffer from the bleached out white hairlines, which so often occur when sunlight affects the filler and bleaches out the colouring.

A classic case of wood veneer deterioration in this early 1970s Jaguar XJ6 saloon. You will have to put in much time to make good, but it *can* be done, as I explain

The wood capping on the front of this Jaguar XJ6 is not only faded, but has been chipped as well. Better to start again, either with new components, or with ambitious re-veneering of your own

Before going any further, though, you must attend to any repairs which are necessary. These may range from quite major glueing operations (where alternate damp and heat has dried out the old glue on sections formed from a number of pieces of wood) to scratches and cigarette burns. Where the wood is solid, use a cabinet maker's scraper, and glasspaper, to get rid of scratches and dents, but where any damage has cut into the veneer, the only feasible method of repairing it is to insert a new section. Veneer to match most types of grain can be obtained from craft shops, which sell it for marquetry work, but it is not always easy to match the colour of the wood when it is dry, as the colour deepens considerably when you apply varnish.

A very close approximation of the varnished colour can be made if you dampen the wood slightly. Though the assistant in the craft shop might look a little askance if you go into the shop carrying a car dashboard, then ask to see a selection of veneers which you can dampen to see whether they match the colour of the dash, it is worth taking the trouble. A patch which ends up as a different colour stands out even more than the original blemish would do.

Putting new veneer on to the edges ought not to present any difficulty, but where the blemish is in the centre of a panel it is not as simple to hide the fact that new veneer is being used. Any cuts which run across the grain of the wood will show up after it is varnished, so if there is some damage, or a cigarette burn, in the centre of a panel, the only way to tackle it with any reasonable chance of success is to cut out an elongated diamond at least two or three inches long with the points of the diamond rounded off across its shorter axis. First cut a patch out of the new veneer, then lay it on top of the panel. Mark it and go round with a sharp craft knife until you have achieved a perfect fit.

The inside of picnic tables, so rarely used, are usually in much better shape than the outsides. At least you can use this as a guide to the true colour of the wood when rebuilding a car

Some purists suggest that because most cars built up to and including the 1950s had woodwork joined together with animal glues, then the same type of glue must be used in the restoration, for authenticity's sake. This is nonsense, and I do not subscribe to such fussiness. I would recommend using a modern resin woodwork adhesive. For a closed car I suggest that you can use the ordinary milky-looking white adhesive, but that for an open car it is advisable to use a waterproof type, because the more normal types will soften when they get wet. If you can handle them, you can use a modern impact adhesive but to my mind this has two disadvantages. One is that it is thick and rubbery and tends to hold joints apart with a slight gap. The other is that once you press the parts together there is no chance for second guessing. In repairing a split or a break there is no chance to push the two parts together, then wriggle them slightly around to obtain a perfect join.

On top quality cars, all the woodwork and veneer should have been matched for colour by the manufacturer when assembly was in progress, but on cheaper cars, and on some others where solid wood was used rather than a veneer, you may find when the old varnish is stripped off that the woodwork may look rather piebald. In some places it could be a fairly deep brown, but in others it may be almost white. If the manufacturer was not too careful in his choice of solid wood, particularly with some of the cheap mahoganies, you may even find that there are light or white coloured streaks running in the grain of a single piece of wood.

When the car was new these were probably all disguised by colouring. The reason that the wood returned more or less to its natural colour when the old varnish was stripped off is that the colouring was in the varnish and not applied to the wood itself. It used to be quite common practice at one time for the workman spraying on the varnish to have two guns, one containing a dark varnish and one containing a medium varnish. He would first cover the lighter panels with the darker varnish, and then—while it was still wet—blend in the medium colour varnish to produce an approximately even colour. Some of the operators using these guns became so skilled, that they could even blend together ordinary white deal and quite dark mahogany.

If you try to do the same thing without a great deal of practice you will probably produce something looking absolutely awful. Fortunately the wood can be brought back to an even colour all over the car in almost every case by using spirit stains. These are much preferable to varnish stains because they sink into the wood and colour it, rather than lie on the surface and merely produce a colouring by reflected light. An alternative to a spirit stain is a water-base stain which some people prefer. Really this is merely a matter of choice.

Some parts of the woodwork may have patches where the varnish has worn off, or been flaked off, and a previous owner of the car may have coloured the wood with some sort of stain. When the rest of the varnish is stripped off, you will see patches darker than the rest. Bleaching out these darker patches is always something of a problem, but there are two methods to be tried. First, use a solution of oxalic acid crystals in warm water, but be careful with the oxalic acid because it is poisonous—keep it well away from children and pets.

You should also be careful when stopping for a meal or sandwich break, if you have oxalic acid on your fingers. It dissolves quite readily in hot water, so normal washing is quite sufficient to get rid of it. It takes from three hours to an overnight halt to do its job of bleaching, and is more effective on some stains than others. An important point is that after using oxalic acid it must be washed absolutely and completely out of the grain of the wood. Merely swabbing down with a damp cloth is not sufficient, as any oxalic crystals left behind will then attack the varnish or any other colouring which is applied. There is only one way to get rid of the acid—by using copious amounts of warm water.

As an alternative to oxalic acid, try using ordinary household bleach in varying dilutions. Sometimes this has a much better effect on some stains than oxalic acid. As with all colouring and bleaching operations, you must try it out first, in fairly dilute form, to see what happens. Once again, it is important to wash out any traces of household bleach thoroughly, before you go on to the next stage.

Other blemishes which may have to be tackled are bruises and dents, oil stains (where someone has lubricated a starter or choke cable), cigarette burns round an ashtray, holes in the woodwork where previous owners have added either extra instruments, or a map reading light and, in the case of solid wood panels, possible splits from fixing screw holes. On veneered woodwork, it may also be necessary to deal with blisters where the veneer has lifted from the base wood.

Bruises and dents can often be 'lifted up' out of the wood by soaking them in hot water, but it is more effective to connect a rubber or plastic pipe to a kettle spout and play the steam locally on to the bruise. Remember that the pipe can become very hot, so be careful how you tackle this job, and always wear some gloves. Steaming will also raise the grain of the wood, as well as raising the bruise, but this can be sanded down afterwards, just so long as you wait until the wood is thoroughly dry—*not* merely dry on the surface.

Oil stains can be a real problem, for many of the penetrating and other oils which people are tempted to use on dashboard controls contain graphite. One can never be sure of complete success in removing oil stains, but the best way to tackle the job is first to get rid of the oil or grease itself (with something like methylated spirit or carbon tetrachloride), and then to try to bleach out whatever colour is left behind. Graphite powder cannot be bleached out, but successive washing with methylated spirit, or rubbing with carbon tetrachloride will often take the graphite away from the top surface of the wood; if you then seal it afterwards with a thinned-down coat of varnish, the chances are that, with luck, the rest of the graphite will stay down in the pores of the wood, and not emerge again.

In veneered panels, the only way to deal with cigarette burns which have charred the wood, is to cut out the veneer and replace it with a new piece, but with solid wood the problem is that the surface of the wood will have been destroyed and no amount of steaming can raise it up again. Try careful application of undiluted household bleach on a small brush, followed by gentle scraping with a razor blade or craft knife to lift out the wood which has been charred beyond recall; then continue with the bleach to try to get rid of the darker stain in the wood which has not actually turned to charcoal. To fill the depression left by getting rid of the charred surface, try using a plastic wood or similar sort of filler but remember that these will react differently to any varnish or stain which you may use later on. Some fillers will even absorb the clear varnish to such an extent that they darken quite considerably—others are completely impervious to any varnish or stain and once they are dry will stay the same colour no matter how they are treated. I recommend that you try out the filler or plastic wood you have chosen on a spare piece of wood, and mix some colouring dye or stain with it, to bring it as near as possible to the colour the finished panel will take on after it is varnished.

As an alternative to using a plastic type of filler, try the old cabinet makers' method of melting shellac into the depression, then scraping it down level with a craft knife or similar sharp blade. Sticks of shellac in various colours can still be obtained from some craft shops, though they are no longer so easy to find as they used to be. If you have difficulty in finding a good filler, or the right colour of shellac stick, try the type of shop which caters for people restoring antique furniture.

Holes and splits in a solid wood panel are almost impossible to disguise. If you are unfortunate enough to have a solid wood dash where a previous owner has cut fairly large holes to take switches or even extra instruments, the only practical solution is to fill the holes with glued-in plugs of wood, and then veneer over the whole surface.

There is nothing difficult about veneering a flat instrument panel. Once you have removed any old varnish which would stop the glue from adhering, coat the surface of the panel with a white resin glue, lay the chosen sheet of veneer on the top, follow this with a sheet of polythene to prevent any glue which squeezes out from sticking to the clamping board, lay a sheet of rubber or fairly hard plastic foam over the top of the polythene, put a board on top of it, and clamp the lot together.

A little more care is needed when you come to trim down the veneer to the edges of the panel. The easiest way is to cut along with a sharp craft knife, or a small model maker's saw, to within about a sixteenth of an inch from the edge, then finish off with sandpaper wrapped round a block, remembering to rub the sandpaper *down* from the top of the veneer to avoid lifting it. If the edges of the panel are to be veneered it is best to do this job before you put the top surface of veneer on, otherwise the edge of the veneer will show as a rim, all the way round the panel.

Smaller blemishes such as screw holes from a map reading light, or nail holes where the original car supplier fixed his advertising plaque, should be filled with coloured shellac and not, as some people say, with a tapered plug of wood. If a plug of wood is pushed in, and then cut down level with the surface, an end grain is left which will soak up any colouring or varnish, then turn darker than the flat surface of the surrounding wood.

Splits from screw holes can be very awkward to repair. No matter how hard you try to clamp the panel together again, the split seldom closes up properly, especially if it has been there for some years. An effective way of dealing with such splits is to gouge them out slightly with some sort of pointed tool—even a screwdriver will do—then insert a piece of veneer into the split, edge on. If a strip of veneer is cut about half an inch wide, then the edge tapered by laying it flat on the bench, and going along with a sandpaper block, it will wedge itself into the split or crack and, helped by a coating of a colourless glue first, it will never be dislodged. When pushing it down into the split, carve it off with a knife just proud of the surface, then tap it down gently with a block of wood. After the glue has dried cut it once again with a craft knife, then sandpaper again, finally to level it.

Once any repairs are finished, rub down the surface again with fine glass-paper; it is now ready for varnishing to start. The type of varnish you choose is really a matter for personal preference, but I have always advised using a clear polyurethane varnish. I have found that it gives a very good finish, and does not deteriorate, nor go cloudy, in strong sunlight, unlike some oil-based varnishes. It has the advantage that a final glass finish can be obtained on it, with a body cleaning compound such as T-cut, followed by a rub with ordinary metal polish. I like to use the water clear varnish which in my opinion, best brings out the

Opposite top **Stripping and washing off will probably have raised the grain, so sand off with very fine paper using a block to avoid rounding the edges of the panel. Be careful you do not cut right through thin veneer**

Opposite bottom **The first few coats of your new varnish will sink in because they are thinned, but gradually you will build up a deep gloss**

grain of the wood, but some people think this looks a little too clinical and they prefer to use one which is tinted slightly yellow. This again, is really a matter of personal choice.

Whichever type of varnish you choose, a much more durable and better finish will result if you thin the varnish well, then apply a large number of thin coats, rather than a small number of coats straight from the tin. I would thin down the varnish at least fifty-fifty with the appropriate thinners, which could be white spirit, or a special thinners made by the manufacturer.

The first two or three coats of varnish seem to have no effect at all, as they will sink right down into the grain, but as you continue with coat after coat—leaving each one to dry first of course—gradually you will build up a smooth

There are bound to be dust marks when the varnish dries, but they can usually be taken out with something like T-Cut. Finish off with metal polish, and wax

surface to the wood. As soon as you see the varnish starts to dry on top of the wood instead of sinking in, let it harden for at least a day, and preferably longer; then work over it with the finest glass-paper you can find. If you can find a cabinet maker's garnet paper, this is even finer than the finest of glass-papers, but it is not very easy to find. Otherwise take the finest grade of glasspaper available and rub two sheets together to take the first harsh cut away from it, otherwise the surface of the varnish will be scratched. Go over the surface lightly until the first coating of varnish which laid on top of the wood has been removed. You should finish up with a completely smooth satin-like surface to the wood with all the pores of the grain filled.

Now you can start to build up the gloss coats. For these I usually thin down the varnish less than for the first few coats used to fill the grain—in some cases only by about ten or fifteen per cent of thinners. If the gloss coats can be sprayed on, so much the better, but if not, the thinned varnish will flow quite easily, and almost all the brush marks will disappear before it begins to set.

To produce a good gloss surface at least four, preferably six coats of varnish will be needed, and I have found that it makes very little difference whether or not the surface is rubbed down between the coats. After the final coat has dried and hardened, and preferably left for at least a couple of days, go over it with very fine—almost worn out—glass paper, rubbing as lightly as possible, merely to take out the nibs and dust marks which will inevitably have formed on the surface.

There should now be a finish to the wood which looks like slightly frosted glass; the final polish and shine can be brought up by using cellulose rubbing compound, a mild abrasive such as metal polish and finally a coating of wax. When you have finished the wood should have an absolutely glass-like surface, which brings out all the beauty and colouring of the wood grain. Even though the finish has hardened it will still be relatively soft for a week or so, so take great care of it and, if you can, avoid fitting the panels back in the car for at least a week, or preferably ten days, to give the varnish a chance to harden thoroughly and absolutely.

Chapter 6 | Upholstery and carpets

The upholstery and side trim panels, once cleaned and repaired, will probably need some extra treatment to bring them back to their best condition. Broadly speaking, upholstery can be divided into three main groups or types; cloth, hide and PVC or Rexine.

Of these, cloth upholstery is probably the most difficult to restore to anything like as-new condition once it has become stained and worn. Probably the best ways of dealing with it are the time honoured methods which have been used for cleaning fabrics—such as using any of the proprietory stain removers and cleaners sold for clothing, and also the milder carpet shampoos.

One of the mistakes you must guard against is to get the upholstery too wet. If you do, and if there is a blue flock padding underneath, there could be a chance of the blue dye coming out of the padding and staining through the cloth. With better quality work this should not be the case as there should be a layer of white padding immediately below the upholstery cloth, but it is as well to make a test on the back edge of a seat or somewhere just to make sure. I would not advise taking off the top covering from the seats for separate washing unless you are particularly expert in handling fabrics, and are absolutely certain that you can wash it without shrinking it. Many cloth upholstery materials used in cars contained a high percentage of wool, especially in higher quality models, and these are notorious for shrinking and for going out of shape.

Velour, whether a natural fibre or man-made type, can often be renovated surprisingly well—first by treating with a degreasing cleaning agent (such as carbon tetrachloride) to get the grease out of the pile so that it does not stick

Opposite **Brushed man-made velour (as on this Rover) wears better than natural fibre, and is easier to clean. Try using ordinary clothes washing preparations to lift out dirt, and 'dry cleaning' fluid for stains**

together, and then going over it with steam and a fairly stiff bristled brush. You will find that the velour usually has a 'nap' or 'flow' to the material which makes it look slightly different in colour when the light shines from different directions. When you are steaming a velour always brush it in the direction in which the pile lies, otherwise when it dries it may look very matted and tangled.

Some cloth materials used in car upholstery have fast colours but others are very fugitive. As well as bleaching out where the sun has played on them (such as along the tops of seats) you may also find that the cleaning agents used to lift out grease and stains also tend to lift out the colour and leave the material looking rather patchy. The best way to deal with this is probably to use a fairly weak solution of ordinary household clothing dye which can be bought from most fabric shops and chainstores. Sponge it on as evenly as possible and let each coat dry before going on to the next. Generally speaking it is better to use a very much weaker solution of the dye than is suggested on the packet for dip dying, and you should therefore give the material several coats.

Rexine and PVC imitation leather upholstery cloths are both man made materials, but the older Rexine was by no means as durable as the more modern PVC. Over the years it rubs to a very shiny surface, and on edges and corners which receive a lot of wear one often finds that the lacquered surface has been rubbed off completely and the finish is down to the fabric base.

There are several ways in which this can be treated. One method is to treat the fabric with any appropriately coloured dye then cover it over with flexible lacquer. Another is to treat the surface with 'leather paint' sold in DIY and craft shops, while a third is to spray it with coloured lacquer normally intended for re-colouring PVC. However, whichever method you choose be very cautious—and try it out initially on a patch which does not show. The reason for this is that some of the more modern plastic based colouring lacquers attack the surface of Rexine and tend to dissolve it.

As an alternative you could try one of the dye-glazes which can be obtained from shoe shops and some shoe

Left **Choose your cleaner carefully for a combination of cloth and vinyl seat covering and if you use a dye on the vinyl be careful not to get it on the cloth. It won't come out!**

Below **For removing small scuffs and scratches, try using a preparation from the shoe shop, but the range of colours is rather restricted**

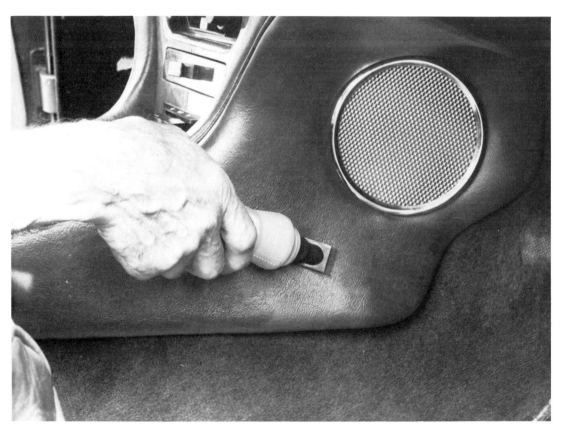

repairers. These are intended for leather and artificial leather, and are usually in two different types. Although they do quite a good job the range of colours is rather restricted so if you are forced to choose a colour which does not match exactly, choose one which is slightly darker than the natural colour of the upholstery.

When it comes to dealing with PVC upholstered seats and trim panels the position is much easier as there are quite a number of preparations on the market for colouring and restoring the surface, usually sold in aerosol can form. One which I have used successfully is made by Sperex and can be found in quite a number of car accessory shops. Once again the range of colours is a little restricted, but the colouring is particularly opaque; and provided you do not try to change a very dark colour to a light colour there will usually be no difficulty at all in getting an even coloured finish all over the seats and panels.

Restoration in tins from Sperex. Most of these products have more than one application in cleaning and refurbishing, but if you experiment, do it first on something that does not matter

Left **It made economic sense to produce complex moulded seat covers like this (the car is a Ford Cortina 1600E), but restoration can be a nightmare if there is damage to overcome. Fortunately, popular cars like this usually have seat covers remanufactured by specialists**

Below **For reviving the surface of vinyl there are several preparations such as this 'Son of a Gun' by STP**

One of the more ticklish jobs for a restorer is to repair the different colour piping on seats, as in this 1965 Triumph Spitfire. On this sort of car, too, the carpets were originally moulded. It is impossible for you to duplicate the contours, but fortunately such 'consumable' items have usually been remanufactured by now

There are several PVC 'revivers', one being sold by Sperex and another is marketed under the brand name of 'Son of a Gun'. All such preparations leave a very high-gloss shine on the PVC, and I believe that most of them contain silicones. On the Sperex and 'Son of a Gun' cans the directions for use instruct you to spray on, or brush on, the liquid then leave it to dry. In the case of the preparations I have tested, I have tried both these methods and that of rubbing on with a cloth—my advice is that cloth application when dried gives the least artificial look. I should warn you to keep these preparations well clear of any PVC or plastic covered steering wheels for these may be rendered extremely slippery and likely to slide through the driver's fingers.

The traditional look of luxury—hide seats and polished wood trim. Though it is often complicated, it is also often easier to refurbish than more modern moulded and padded trim

Some Jaguars, Humbers and other makes used a mixture of genuine hide and PVC in their cars. In some cases the seats are upholstered in hide and the trim panels in PVC, and in other cases one may also find the backs of the front seats upholstered in PVC. Make sure you identify which is which, because some of the preparations which are very beneficial when treating PVC can have an absolutely disastrous effect on a lacquered hide surface, although the materials used for treating hide are far less likely to have any bad effect on PVC.

More than ninety per cent of all the upholstery hide used on British cars has been supplied by Connolly Brothers, the company claims. It is still very much of a family firm, and I have always found them a most helpful and efficient

Right **The combination of old and new in a 1960s Jaguar Daimler results in polished wood but with moulded crash padding and non-projecting switches. The mouldings are difficult to repair if they become torn as the material is stuck to the foam, but you can sometimes re-cover over the old material**

Below **Leather covered steering wheels can be re-covered at home but doing it by hand is a finger-aching job. Most trim shops will re-cover a wheel like this at surprisingly small cost**

company to deal with. The company has recently moved its premises, and its full title and new address is Connolly Brothers (Curriers) Limited, Wandle Bank, Wimbledon, SW19 1DW. In the United States, Connolly's agents are the Pacific Hide and Leather Co. Inc. of 1400 South Broadway, Los Angeles, California, and William S. Hirsch of 396 Littleton Avenue, Newark, New Jersey.

If you send a snippet of unfaded hide to Connolly, or its agents, cut it from somewhere such as under the seat where it will not be noticed. They can usually then supply a dye and a lacquer, as well as a hide food, to bring the seats back to very nearly new condition. I have visited their premises in Wimbledon and watched their own craftsmen restoring old car seats. Provided that the glazed surface of the hide is not cracking and flaking, the results are always extremely good.

They recommend using only a pure soap for the first cleaning of the hide, so that there is no chance of any chemicals being left behind which might affect the dye. Sponge on the dye, which looks rather like a thin enamel paint, quite liberally to the surface of the hide, using long even strokes, then leave it to dry. If there is a contrasting edging or piping to the seats this can be picked out either before or afterwards (or both) by using a small paint brush. The dye dries reasonably quickly, and dries with a fairly soft gloss which I find much more pleasing than the high gloss produced by most of the PVC restorers and colouring sprays. After it has dried, which takes two or three hours, start feeding hide food into the surface, which once again is obtainable from Connollys, and finish off with a soft cloth.

Moving now to the carpets, there is little, if anything, that can be done to rescue a carpet which has worn threadbare. Probably the best method, short of replacement, is to use a cloth dye to make the carpet an even colour all over then leave it at that. Renewing the edging or binding round the sections of carpet often makes it look very much better as these are the parts which often wear and 'kick up' when the stitching becomes rotten.

If you decide to replace the carpet, you have the choice in most cases of buying a set of carpets ready tailored for

Above **No matter how tatty a carpet is, don't throw it—or indeed any piece of trim—away before you have made its replacement**

Right **On this type of carpet with an open weave you must coat the back with adhesive along the cutting line before you actually cut. If you do not, it will fray for at least half an inch or so**

Above **At many autojumbles you may find 'new old stock' of upholstery panels ready made, as well as rolls of carpet, headlining material and most of the fittings you need. This is part of the stock of Befour Conversions Limited of Waltham Abbey, Essex**

Left **To make a sewn seam in a carpet, hold the two pieces with the piles together and oversew the seam. It will then flatten out when you unfold the carpet**

your car, or of buying the carpeting material by the metre and making new ones up for yourself.

Buying new ready-made carpet is not always quite so simple a solution as it seems, for the carpeting in even quite a small car is often made up of so many small bits and pieces that it is quite a jigsaw puzzle problem to fit in the new pieces. To guard against pieces being slightly too small, many suppliers of tailored carpets leave such pieces as the side kick panels in the front, the pieces over the wheel arches at the rear, and any trim in the back of an estate car or in the boot of a saloon, rather larger than is necessary so there may be some trimming down to be done.

This is not particularly difficult as the carpet is always supplied with a non fraying coating fixed to the back so that it can be cut quite easily using a sharp knife or even a heavy pair of carpet layer's scissors. Where panels are not handed (that is where one is able to fit them either to the left or right of a car) make sure you choose the side

When taking out carpets, underfelt, and other trim items from a floor pan or footwell, be sure you know how they ought to 'lay up' when you come to re-assemble around the corners of curved pieces like the gearbox tunnel

on which to fit them so that the pile of the carpet runs in the same direction as the pile on the main carpeting of the floor, otherwise the result can look odd.

In most cases the carpet is fixed down to the floor either by press studs or 'Lift-the-Dot' fasteners which can be obtained at most shops which cater for car trim and upholstery. In the case of side panels and coverings over wheel arches the carpet is usually stuck down. Buy an adhesive to do the job from the same shops which sell the carpet fasteners; one of the best adhesives I have encountered is made by the 3M Company, while another good one is made by Dunlop.

To cut new carpets from a roll, either because you have made this choice or because a tailored set for your car is nowhere to be found, first take out all the old carpets, open up any seams, then lay them out on a large flat area—even on the lawn if the weather is favourable. Label the pieces as they are removed, so that you will know their location

Even a carpet like this is valuable for providing a pattern for the new one, but it is badly frayed at the outer edge. Stains can be cleaned out, but such fraying is really impossible to make good

A puzzle for the restorer. Does the handbrake have to be dismantled before the carpets can be removed? Are the tunnel carpets stuck down by adhesive, or will lifting the side panels reveal some more secure method. One consolation is that the centre console of this Big Healey can be unclipped very quickly indeed

in the car, because the most economical way to cut into a roll may not always be obvious until all the carpets are laid out together. Be careful to get the nap of the pile running correctly.

Make a careful note of how the joins and seams, such as those which cover the gearbox hump, are made, so that when the new pieces are cut there is a reasonable chance of getting them into the right shape. The old carpet will certainly have stretched and produced humps in places, but usually it is possible to tell from the weave at the back whether or not it is a seam, a tuck, or whether it has merely stretched; cut the new carpet accordingly.

When joining seams and vee-cuts in the new carpet there are several ways of joining the edges, depending on the type of carpet chosen. In any case, choose the type of carpet which does not fray at the edges as soon as it is cut. Be careful when inspecting the carpet because some carpets do not fray when cut across the roll but when cut down the roll they become frayed at the edges quite readily.

If the carpet has a woven back, you can either sew or stick the edges together, then reinforce the back of the join with a strip of carpet binding stuck into place. Sticking the carpet in the joints is quite a tricky business, mainly because one must be very careful not to smear the adhesive onto the top surface. There are various brand names of carpet adhesive, one of the most popular being Copydex, but several others are just as effective. Probably the easiest way is to cut a piece of carpet binding to reinforce the back of the join, put the adhesive on the back of the carpet at one side of the join, stick this down to the binding and then put the adhesive for the second edge onto the binding itself before bringing the two together. Then fold the join so that the gap at the pile side is open and, being very careful, put some adhesive in the join with a child's small paint-

This is a good workaday classic car, with serviceable carpets. Notice, however, that the lay-up, and fitting, of the carpets and the trim round the door pillar is quite complicated. When getting ready to strip out, either make sketches of such fittings, and number the trim as it comes out, or take Polaroid pictures as an aide-memoire

brush; finally bring the join together again so that the actual edges of the carpet and the bottom part of the pile stick together.

With a rubber backed carpet one must choose the adhesive carefully so that the carpet binding will stick properly. When buying the adhesive consult the shop where you bought the carpet, and get an assurance that the two are compatible.

In the case of a carpet with a fabric woven back, the alternative to sticking the joins is to sew the edges of the join together. To do this, fold the vee-cut so that the pile is inside and the fabric backing is outside—or if they are two separate pieces, lay the two pieces of carpet together—and run a small screwdriver or something similar through the edge so that all the pile is pushed down and none is left sticking up between the two fabric woven parts of the join.

Then, work along the join with a fairly heavy needle and waxed linen thread, oversewing rather than sewing backwards and forwards, and pulling the thread really tight as progress is made. Every four or five stitches take the needle back on itself so that a knot is formed in the stitching. This makes it much less likely that the join will gape in places because the thread pulls through to one end. When the join is unfolded it will probably look much more like a deep vee than a nice flat join, but with a little coaxing and maybe folding over a curved edge, it will flatten down as the edges of the carpet settle down on the linen thread.

There are again two methods to use when it comes to binding the edges of the carpet. The first, which is the simplest and which is used on most cheaper carpets, is merely to fold the edge binding over the edge of the carpet and sew straight through. The second way, which is much neater and which is usually used on top quality work, is to sew it with 'invisible' stitches. Sew the edge binding twice. For the first operation lay it on top of the carpet, face side down, then run a line of stitching along the edge of both the binding and the carpet, about a half an inch from the edge. Then fold the binding back on itself, over the edge of the carpet, so that the line of the stitches is hidden, fold it down over the back of the carpet and sew it to the back with blind stitches. Make these blind stitches

Often a good clean and new edge binding will transform the looks of a carpet. Once again this binding is just sewn on, but to make a neater job you can blind sew it (see text)

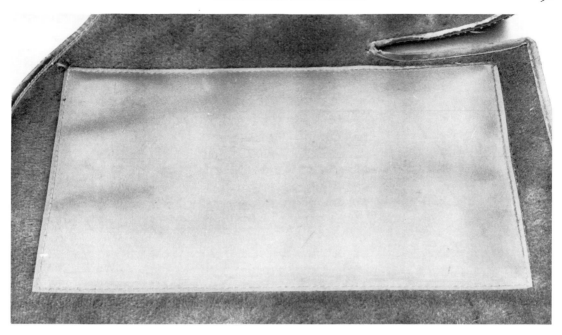

with a curved needle so that the thread just goes into the fabric back of the carpet and not through into the pile. This is a much longer, and in some ways much more finger-aching job than plain sewing, but it is worth the trouble if you are looking for a really neat finish to the edges of the carpet.

The original carpet will often have had a rubber panel let into it under the driver's heels; these rubber pads can be found in most car trim and upholstery shops. They are specially made for the job in that the ribbed pattern stops near the edges to leave about a quarter of an inch, or sometimes half an inch, of plain rubber. Cut a hole in the carpet to the exact size of the ribbed part, and then place the rubber matting in place from the back so that the plain edge lies on the back part or underside of the carpet.

With a rubber backed carpet put the rubber matting in place with an adhesive. Sometimes this is also successful with a woven back carpet, but, in the case of a carpet with a woven back, I would prefer to reinforce the adhesive with a few very small stitches run round the edge. It is none too easy to push a needle through the heavy black rubber

A rubber or plastic heel pad helps to prevent wear on the front carpets. This one is just sewn on top of the pile, but on top quality cars, they were let into the carpet

of these heel mats, so you might find it useful to make the holes with an awl or similar pointed tool before pushing the needle through.

At this stage, to minimize noise levels inside the car, put a sound deadening layer underneath the carpet. The best results will be obtained if you use a specific sound deadening material rather than just an ordinary underfelt. Usually such sound deadening material is made in plastic foam which has a smooth surface on one side. Check with the foam manufacturer first to make sure, but in most cases you will find that it is intended to be laid on the floor with the smooth side upwards, not down against the metal. The idea is that the foam absorbs and dampens down the noise and vibrations which come up through the floor, and the smooth layer reflects the dampened vibrations back down through the layer to stop them coming up into the car.

Such sound deadening material is usually quite thick and if you try to use the normal type of short shank carpet fastener you will find some difficulty. In the trim shop try to find the longer type of shank fasteners which are specially made to be used with an underlay.

It does no harm at all to put a layer of this sound deadening material round the body panels of the car underneath the trim panels, and also in the doors provided it does not get in the way of the movement of the window winding mechanism. Before sticking it into place on the body panels or onto the inside of the doors, treat the metal surfaces with a couple of good coats of paint followed by one of underbody sealing compound so that, should the sound deadening material hold any water which has come down through the window channelling, it will not form rust patches on the door. In some cases, you will find that existing sound deadening material has a sheet of polythene put over it, which is fastened down to the inside panel of the door by strips of adhesive tape, so that any water which does find its way down past the window runs straight down to the bottom and out of the door drainholes, instead of collecting in the sound deadening foam. Once again, ask in the trim shop for the adhesive tape. This is a much stronger type of tape than the sort you buy in the normal high street shop, and has a much more powerful adhesive.

Take a layer of the sound deadening material all the way up the scuttle/firewall behind the dash, and also down the back panel between the passenger compartment of the car and the boot, as well as under the rear seat. To make the car even quieter you could also use the sound deadening material on the roof, under the headlining. The main idea is to dampen down noise reflections inside the car so that any noise which comes in the car is damped to a low frequency and is soon absorbed by the carpet, upholstery and trim. Some shops offer kits of thick felt, already tailored to suit your car, at a much lower price than you have to pay for the proper sound deadening foam, but these are not as effective. If you have trouble in finding a good sound deadening material, try Sound Services Limited, of Witney in Oxfordshire.

Although a tonneau cover looks complicated, it all started life as a series of flat pieces of material. Either have a new one made up, if necessary, or make piece by piece copies, yourself, of the old cover still with your car. You may be forced to use old zips in the new item

Chapter 7 | Door trim and panels

The parts of the trim most likely to be in bad condition, and most likely to need replacing, are the interior door trim panels. They take many a kick from people getting into and out of the car, and the water which inevitably finds it way down past the window tends to rot and warp the bottom of the panel itself, which in many cases is made from a cheap compressed cardboard. Sometimes, in trim shops, you will find replacement panels of the same compressed cardboard, which are ready cut to size. It is a quick way of replacing the panel, but these are available for only a relatively limited number of models; if you are unlucky you will probably have to make the new panel yourself. Buy the sheets of the compressed card from which to cut new panels, and use the old panel as a pattern. As an alternative make them out of fairly thin resin bonded marine

New carpeting will give a new look to the floor and seat back of many estates, but unfortunately the fibre board side trim panels on this car are moulded. Such panels are easily damaged and may sometimes warp as they age. You may have to use some ingenuity with stiffeners behind the fibre board to get them into shape again

Left **Some restoration companies stock replacement trim panels ready cut, but if not you will have to make your own from fibre board or thin resin bonded plywood**

Below **You often meet this sad sight when you take the door trim off. The only cure is to make up a complete new trim panel though with luck you can use the original covering again**

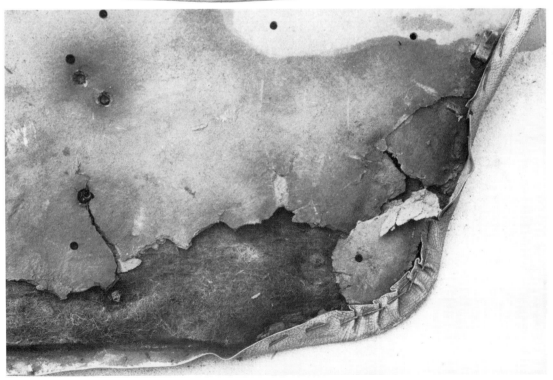

quality plywood, for this lasts very much longer. The spring clips for the blind fastening of door trim panels usually go rusty. They are quite cheap to buy in car upholstery and trim shops, so I do not think it is worth trying to economize on them, but make sure that you can get new clips of the right size *before* you throw the old ones away.

Right **This plywood was not resin bonded and is part of a moulded panel, but with luck in a case like this you can strip it out without damaging the covering**

Below **Parcel shelves in the front often lead a hard life and tend to sag. Usually the only answer to bring them back to look like this is to renew the shelf under the covering**

Where there is a cloth or leather capping rail to the door trim you will sometimes find a tacking strip of wood underneath. Often this is bedded in Mastik to stop leaks

On cheaper cars the trim material, usually of Rexine or PVC, was stuck straight down to the panel, and merely folded over the edges. This does the job well enough, but if you want a much better, slightly 'plump' look to the door panels which makes the car look so much more luxurious, put a thin layer of linter's felt onto the panel before putting the covering over the top. Linter's felt is a white fluffy material rather like cotton wool, and if the car upholstery shop does not keep it, try a shop which supplies upholsterers of ordinary furniture. Even in these days of plastic foam filling it is very widely used for household cushions and furniture. If you have real difficulty getting it try a shop which caters for furniture restorers. Buy linter's felt in a roll, and hold it in place on the panel with a few dabs of adhesive before putting the covering on.

Both **The centre console of a
Jaguar E type 'basket case' looks
complex—until you turn over and
see just how little is actually
involved. Most of the trim is
stuck down direct to the steel
foldings**

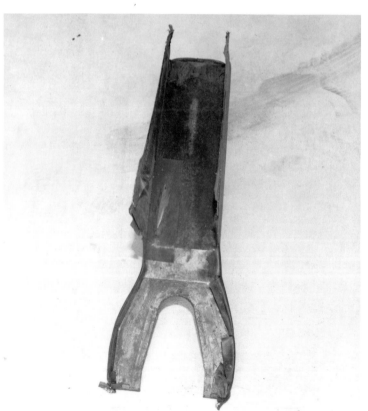

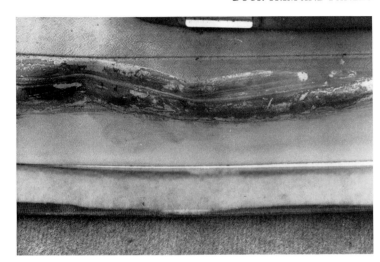

Left **A layer of soft fluffy linter's felt under the door trim gives it a plump luxury look**

Below **By comparison with the TA, the MG TF of 1953 was a more complex trim job. However, it was easy to get at everything from the under-side of the dashboard. If trim panels are missing from an old car of this type, you should be able to inspect someone else's example to see how the finished job should be**

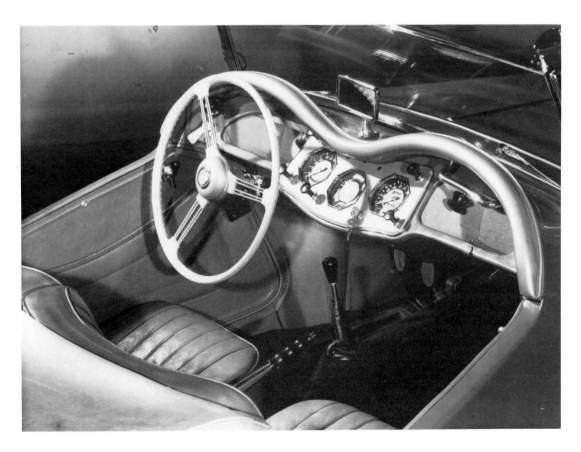

Even though the adhesive dried out long ago, the staples held this trim in place and, from the front, nothing looked amiss

It is often easier to fix the covering to one of the straight edges of the panel, then put the linter's felt on and fold the covering over it, rather than to try to lay the covering loosely over the top of the felt and pull it down at the sides. Use an adhesive (the same one as used for the carpet on the wheel arches will probably do very well) to hold the trim material to the back of the panel.

Most of these adhesives are of the impact type. Spray both surfaces, let them dry and then press them together. They stick almost instantaneously, but because they have a rubbery sort of consistency there is always a tendency for the material to creep sideways so that it sags or goes loose on the top of the panel. To prevent this, you will find that in many cases the original trim was held to the back of the panel by staples as well as by adhesive. Most DIY shops stock a staple gun which will do the job, but be very careful about the length of the legs on the staples which you choose. It is possible to buy staples with very short legs so that they do not come through the other side of the panel and eventually wear a hole through the trim covering.

Start by fixing the covering in the centres of the edges and work your way out towards the corners. When working at the corners there will obviously be too much material

Both **Two views of a very simple type of door trim panel, actually from an MG MGC. Apart from the welded crease panels, you should be able to reproduce and trim such a panel yourself**

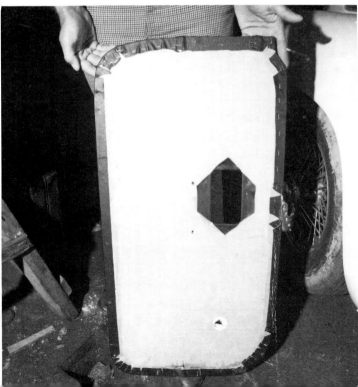

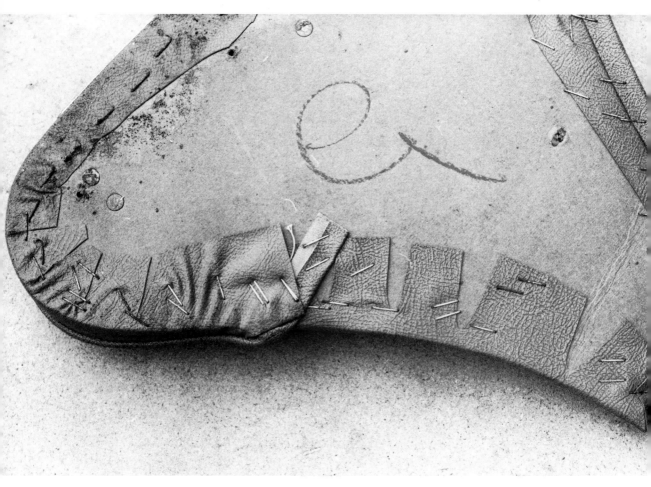

For shaping trim round a sharp curve you will have to make vee-cuts in the trim. Note the staples to hold it in place

over the back to get it flat so you will need to make a series of vee-cuts as you go round. You are most likely to get a smooth, even curve by fixing the middle of the corner after coming along the sides, and then spreading the vee-cuts evenly round the curve. If you start from one side of the corner and try to work your way round, you will probably find that some excess trim material is left over when you get back onto the straight edge again. Make a number of small vee-cuts rather than just two or three large ones, spread round the curve. Make the other interior trim panels, such as those which run round the insides of the door pillars or on the back quarters, in the same way.

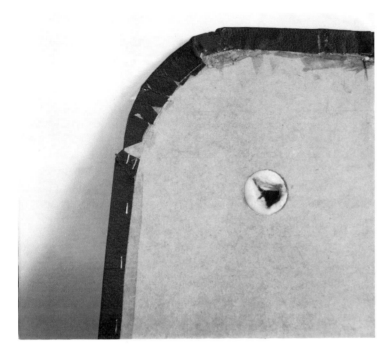

The MG MGC door trim panel is based on a type of fibre board. The corners of the trim are cut carefully, and partly stapled, partly stuck down. To give a bit of richness to the feel of the panel, there is a layer of padding between vinyl trim and fibre board, visible around the edge of the cut out for the winding handle

For trimming around the hole for the inside door handle, nothing more elaborate than this method is needed

Cars which have armrests and pockets in the doors are a little bit more awkward to deal with but, provided you take the old trim panel apart carefully and make a note of how each piece fits to its neighbour, you should not have any real difficulties.

Some armrests are fixed directly to the trim panel and in most cases where the trim panel has begun to buckle the armrest has helped it to promote this. In most cases the armrests were fixed to the trim panel by screws from the back, and it is worthwhile investigating whether there is space between the trim panel and the window when it is lowered, to put a reinforcing panel behind the main trim panel so the load of the armrest is spread.

If you find armrests held to the fibre board door trim merely by screws and large washers, the panel will probably have bowed. Replace the washers by a reinforcing plate

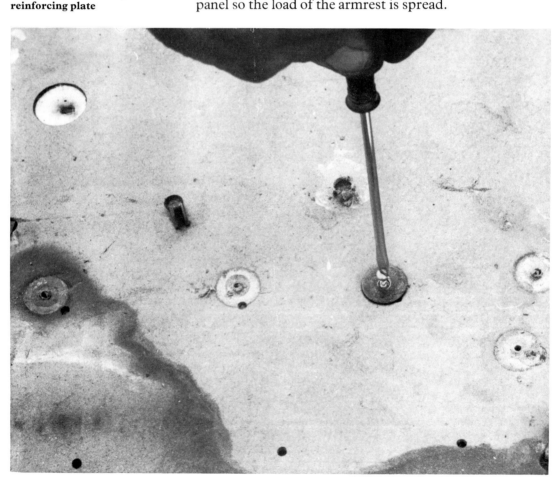

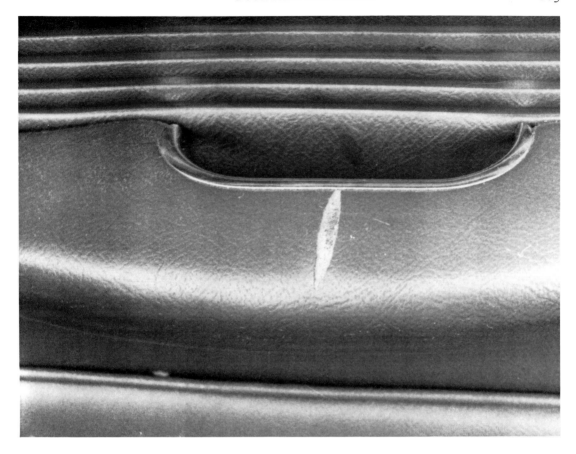

The most difficult type of armrest to cope with is that which began to appear in the late 1960s and which has the PVC covering 'hot-pressed' over a block of moulded foam. It is almost impossible for you to reproduce the shape and seamless contour of the PVC covering by sewing a separate covering to fit over the moulded foam. For complete authenticity the best way, if yours is damaged, is to look for a secondhand one in better condition at a breakers' yard or an autojumble. Some armrests are adjustable for height on a pair of tracks very similar to a seat adjustment, and the method of fixing them and putting a new spring in the latch is usually quite easy to sort out.

A nasty split in the covering of an armrest. As the component is moulded, it is easier to replace the complete rest, even if it means using a dye to change the colour, than try to make what might seem to be a simple repair

Above **On a moulded dash with
crash padding, a chip in the
moulded vinyl is very difficult to
repair. You could try letting a
piece in, but if you can find a
better dash or top rail it is often
easier to change them over**

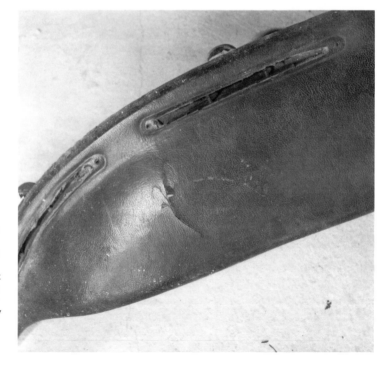

Right **The split in the trim of this
Jaguar E type fascia crash roll is
very bad news for the restorer, as
the vinyl is stuck to a foam
former, and you cannot really get
a patch in underneath to disguise
the split. If you cannot find a new
component, it might be necessary
to have the whole crash roll
recovered with cosmetically-
correct material**

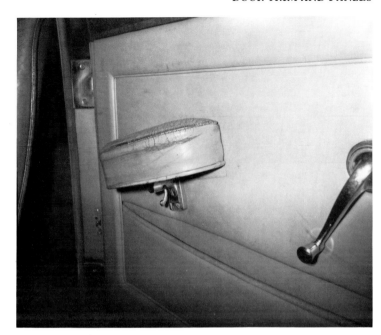

Left **The armrest of this R type Bentley has badly cracked leather covering. Clean it up, then treat the cracking as the patina of age, if you must, otherwise face up to have the moulded component recovered**

Below **Some door pockets are quite simple and held by an elastic strap like this. Others are less obvious, so make sure you know what makes the flap return before you start pulling things to pieces**

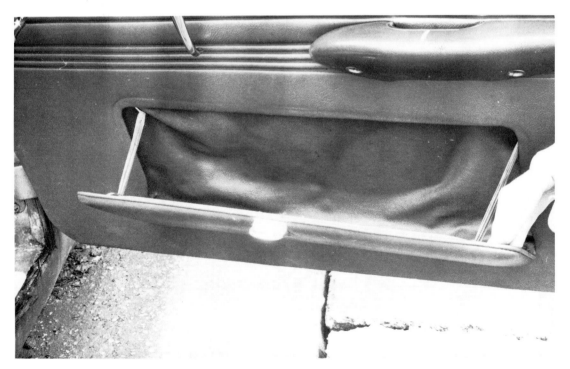

Box type door pockets at the bottom of the door, very often with the inside face covered by carpet, should present no difficulties, but many home restorers fight shy of the type of door pocket which has an elasticated top. Once again, the best way to make a new one is to take the old one carefully to pieces, then use it as a pattern for cutting out the new material. There are two ways of providing the elasticated top, the simple way in which the top of the pocket is folded over and sewn and the elastic threaded through, and the slightly more difficult way—often used on higher priced cars—where the elastic is sewn into the fold so that it gathers in a series of even creases. In this case the elastic, often a wide ribbon of elastic, has to be stretched while it is being sewn in. Any good book on domestic sewing techniques will give you the method.

On this bucket type door pocket, the stitching has not come undone, as you might think, but the fibre board has warped. Sometimes you can stiffen it from inside by using a strip of wood or metal

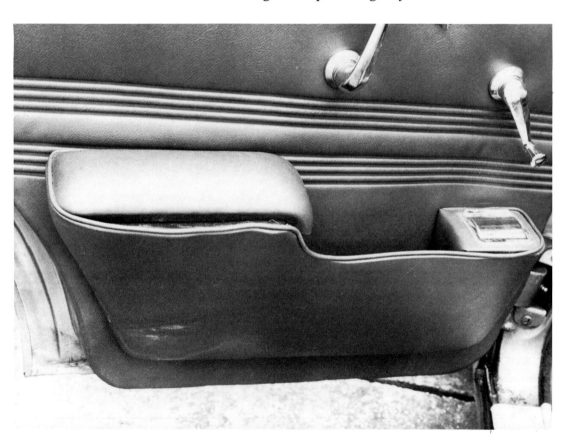

If you decide to have a new tonneau, or hood, made up, try to work out the 'dressmaking' aspect of it all, to see which small sections have to be sewn into larger sections, and be sure that you can locate enough of the correct type of fixings

Most heavy duty domestic sewing machines will handle two or three layers of PVC, but many of them baulk at the idea of handling thicker hide. Some of the lighter domestic sewing machines do not like handling even three layers of PVC cloth. Since damaging the machine and having it repaired would probably be more expensive than having the trim pockets or other parts of sewn upholstery, produced by a trim shop, (not to mention the domestic disharmony that might be caused!) if you plan to retrim the complete interior it is a good idea to look out for a second heavy-duty sewing machine, which is often called an industrial type of machine.

These were made for a much heavier duty than the ordinary domestic machine, and even the older ones are usually still capable of doing very good work. Often the only reason they have been pensioned off, is that they have been superseded by more modern and faster electric machines. You may have to hunt and ask for them—for example the Singer agent in my town had two of them tucked away in a back room and did not bother about them until a couple of local enthusiasts made enquiries. They bought the two for £25 and found that both were in quite good working order.

Before you buy an older industrial type of sewing machine, make sure that the needles are still available for it and that it has a reasonable supply of bobbins. Also, try to get hold of some large spools of 'industrial thread' which is much stronger than ordinary dressmaking cotton, but not quite so thick as button thread. It is much less likely to snap when you are sewing heavy materials, and will go through the machine more easily than button thread, which often contains rough joins along it which jam in the needle.

Headrests present an added complication (as on this MGB), but if you need to repair the covering it usually comes off after undoing a row of stitching at the back. Watch out though, for moulded covering stuck to a foam base. This will not come off

Without an industrial sewing machine, you will have to resort to hand sewing of the heavier materials. This is a long, finger-aching job, but it can be done. The usual method is to use two needles, one fixed to each end of a length of thread, and to start at the end of the seam with the middle of the thread in the middle. Then each needle is passed alternately from either side of the material through the same hole so that the finished sewing looks rather like a line of machine stitching. To help space the stitching evenly most leathercraft shops sell a stitch marker which looks like two or more old fashioned spiked spur wheels on the end of a handle. Depending on what spacing stitching you want, run one of the wheels along the seam to mark the holes for the stitches. These marking wheels are not intended to punch holes in thick material such as hide, for they are only markers; to make the job easier on your fingers it is best to go along afterwards and enlarge the holes slightly with a fine round awl which, if you cannot find one in the shop, can be made quite easily by putting a wooden handle on the end of a heavy duty needle. Rubbing a block of beeswax along the thread will make it pull through hide much more easily as well as helping to preserve it from rotting, and will make it less likely to catch up in tangles.

Chapter 8 | Tackling a headlining

Many home restorers fight shy of making a complete new headlining. However, provided you go about it in a methodical way there is nothing particularly difficult, if you have access to a heavy duty sewing machine which will handle the material.

Various ways of fixing the headlining have been used over the years, ranging from a metal framework to which the headlining is fixed (before it is sprung into position) to the much more elaborate woolcloth type where the headlining is made up of a number of pieces each fixed separately to the inside of the car. Take down the old headlining carefully and make a note of how each part of it is fixed. Start from the bottom edges which were under the side trim panels, and which may be tacked to a wooden strip running round the car or, more likely, are just held to the inside of the bodywork with a few dabs of adhesive.

Sometimes these side headliner or curtain panels were sewn into the main headlining, but sometimes they were fixed separately. In most cases where they are fixed separately there is a second wooden tacking rail running round the edge of the roof and the side panels had a false piping between them and the main headlining cloth. After lifting up the side panels you will often find a strip of thin cardboard used as a tacking strip so that when the side panel is folded down over it, it gives a sharp clean edge to the top rather than one which sags in a series of bows between the tacks.

Be careful how you remove the tacks. Tack lifters of the type which look rather like a screwdriver blade with a vee-cut in the end, are not the easiest tools to use. Most professional trimmers use an old wide bladed chisel run

Both **How to strip away the trim, and headlining of this car? Start by unscrewing the brightwork finishers, the interior lamp, coat hooks, sun vizors and other details, then all should be revealed**

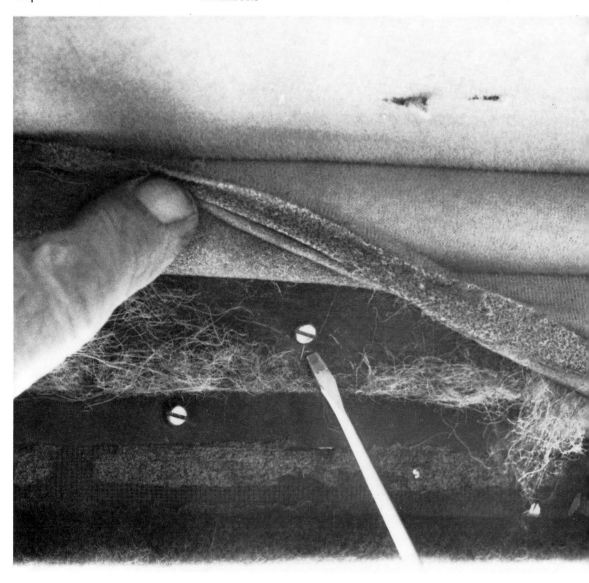

As you lift up successive edges to the headlining you are likely to come across hidden screws such as these

underneath all the layers of cloth fairly flat against the wooden tacking strip, and tap it along gently under the heads of the tacks. This method usually lifts them out quite cleanly and is less likely to damage the wooden tacking strip than by gouging away from the top with a screwdriver or tack lifter.

The headlining of this Riley RM saloon is in three sections—the large centre piece, and the two side pieces, one of which also surrounds the interior lamp and support. To strip down, start from the edges

Where there are no wood tacking strips the sides of the headlining may be supported by a rod or a metal strip which runs along a pocket sewn at the edge of the headlining, or they may be held by a flexible wire fixed to a bolt somewhere at the back of the car and running along a groove in the bodywork and finally down the windscreen pillar towards the front. The fixing points for such wires are not very obvious and you may have to grope about under the dash to find the front one (see chapter 2). To support the centre part of the main lining there are sometimes wooden tacking strips which run across the car, and sometimes sprung-in metal strips or metal rods.

In the first case, a tacking strip of canvas or calico was sewn into the headlining, and in the second case a pocket into which the metal strip fitted was sewn in. When making the new lining it is important to get the transverse seams for these absolutely parallel, though in most cases the actual distance apart of the seams is not critical to within half an inch or so. At the rear quarters of some luxury cars you will find tacking tapes sewn in so that the headlining can be pulled back into the corner, but on most cheaper cars it ran round in a smooth curve.

As with velour materials and carpets, some woolcloth headlinings have a short pile or nap, and it is important when cutting the new headlining to make sure that the nap all runs in the same direction. Check on the old headlining before you take it apart. In some cases where these nap headlinings were used the nap ran from front to back on the main panel and vertically downwards (i.e. sideways) on the side panels, but in some cases it ran from front to back on all the panels. The slightly cheaper type of wool headlining cloth has no nap at all so it does not matter much how you cut out the material, except to watch for different degrees of stretch along and across the material.

When taking the old headlining down and out of the car, take the seams apart carefully, and use the old lining as a pattern for cutting the new one. Then, when you come to refit, put it back together in the reverse order of taking it out. If there are supporting tacking rails running across the roof start with one of these near the middle and then work your way alternately from front to back pulling the headlining evenly and fairly tightly as you go. In the case of sprung-in transverse rods or metal strips there will sometimes be a slot in the side of the body to which they fit, and in other cases they merely spring in and rely on the grip of the rod or strip on the channels to provide the tension in the headlining. Many of the metal rods and strips were originally wrapped in wax paper to guard against stains on the headlinings when they went rusty—as they inevitably do, from condensation—and in most cases you will find this waxed paper in pretty poor condition. If there is rust on any of the headlining frame or tension rods, clean it off, give the rod a coat of paint and, when it is dry, wrap ordinary PVC tape round it. This will keep any rust at bay for years and make it much less likely that anything will come through to stain the lining cloth.

On many smaller cars, the headlining is fixed to a frame which lifts out from grooves in the side of the body

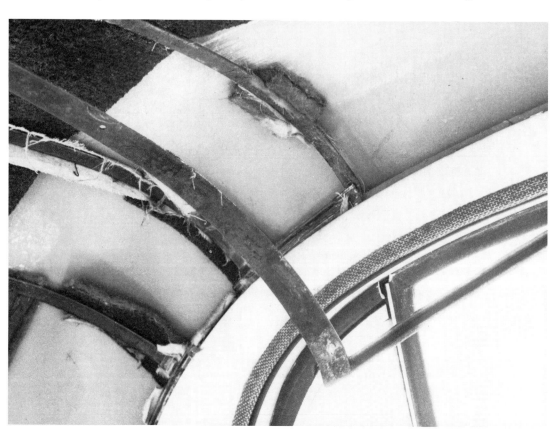

A suitable case for treatment—the headlining and quarter trim panels of a Jaguar XJ6, which will all respond to careful cleaning

Whether you intend to tack or to fix the sides of the strip with adhesive, either use widely spaced tacks or dabs of adhesive first, until the headlining is fully in position. If you immediately go along with a close row of tacks, or a continuous band of adhesive, you will find it very difficult to adjust the headlining to get rid of any wrinkles. When you have the headlining as taut and wrinkle free as possible, that is the time to finish off the fixing.

The covering for this sun visor was blind sewn on the 'wrong side' and then turned inside out like a glove

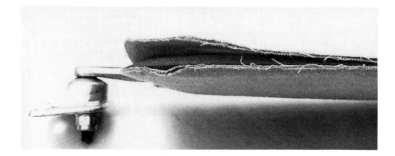

An accessory—Weathershields, actually—sunroof fitted to an MGC GT. How can it be removed? Look, and probe, before you start to unscrew, but generally this method should be clear

With a plastic headlining there is little you can do to alter it once it is up, but with a woolcloth headlining an old trimmers' trick to bring it up very taut is to use steam from a kettle with a rubber or plastic pipe on the spout. Leave the last fixing at the sides, or the fixing where the roof light is mounted, open, and poke the plastic or rubber tube up inside the headlining to play steam round the inside. There is no need to overdo it so that the headlining

After removing a sun-roof to renovate the bodywork, I recommend that you seal it back to the bodyshell with Seelastic, or a similar compound

becomes soaking wet, for a fairly light steaming is all that is necessary. Remember that this is just a final shrinking of a woolcloth to make it evenly taut, but it will not take out any wrinkles. Indeed you often find the reverse is the case in that it will make any wrinkles more noticeable as the headlining shrinks.

Sunshine roofs often present a problem, not because they are difficult to line, but because the method of taking them in and out is not always obvious. So many different designs of sunshine roof have been used over the years that it is quite impossible to describe them all here, but generally speaking either look for side runners which can be loosened when the roof is slid back (so that, when the frame is slid forward it can be lifted out over the front) or look for hidden fasteners under the lining of the roof. Sometimes these hidden fasteners were made rather like bolts or latches which were pushed into engagement after the sunroof was put in position. In some other cases you find that when the rocking handle for the roof is turned and its fixing screws undone, it will take another quarter turn to unlock the side bars completely from the framework.

Chapter 9 | Finishing details

Attention to the smaller details in the interior will finally set off and complement all the hard work you have put into refurbishing the seats, carpets, headlining and trim panels. In some cases refurbishing the details is just a simple matter of cleaning but in others you have to replace.

Weather strips round the edges of door apertures usually need replacing as they will have been kicked and rubbed over the years. More modern cars usually have a plain rubber moulding, but on the earlier postwar cars it was quite common for the draught excluder, as it was usually termed, to be a cloth-covered piping usually with a rubber tube on the inside. In some trim shops you may find ready made draught proofing in plain colours, and sometimes on models where there is enough demand, you will be able to find ready made draught excluder in velour or in moquette to match the interior of the car. If none is available, these piped draught excluders are not very difficult to make, provided you choose the material carefully. Feeding them round the corners of the door aperture without either wrinkling or cutting across the corner can sometimes be a problem, but it can be eased by cutting the strips of material on the bias—diagonally across the weave. With most cloth materials this gives the material the best chance of stretching in either direction and makes it considerably easier to feed neatly it into the corners.

Sometimes the draught excluder round the door was held by being tucked under the side panels and the headlining and fastened either with tacks, clips or an adhesive, but on later models you may find that it usually pushes straight on to a welded bodywork seam with a metal spring clip plate running the whole length of the rubber interior

Don't lose anything, and never throw anything away! We 'borrowed' this valuable little tinfull of fixing bracketry from an experienced trimmer to illustrate the infuriating, but necessary, little items which you will always need, and which make restoration of an incomplete car such a long-winded business

The interior of many glove boxes is sprayed with flock on to an adhesive. Sometimes an electrostatic charge was used to make the flock stand on end like a pile. You cannot reproduce this at home, but try covering worn sprayed flock with a flock surfaced material held in by adhesive

Rubbed and worn draught strip and trim round a door aperture looks very tatty and is usually fairly easy to replace

to the draught excluder. Once these spring strips either rust or are bent they never grip satisfactorily again, but fortunately they are relatively easy to obtain from trim shops, even if they are intended for a much later model than the one being restored. In some cases a draught excluding strip of this type intended for a later model can be modified and covered with cloth to make it fit very much older cars.

At the bottom of the door there is often an aluminium kick plate with a chequer design on it, and sometimes with the make of the car embossed or moulded into it. The best way to clean these plates is to use one of the brightening liquids (which can be found in almost every accessory shop) intended for brightening magnesium alloy wheels. After the plate is thoroughly clean, wash off all the cleaning chemical, dry it thoroughly and give it a couple of coats of water-clear polyurethane varnish to keep it bright. Aluminium does not corrode in the accepted sense that steel corrodes, but it does develop a protective layer of aluminium oxide very quickly; in time this layer goes dull and gives the aluminium a flat, rather frosted, look. It is a nice touch on these kick plates, and indeed, on any panels or finishers

Draught excluding strip to match almost any car, as found at an autojumble

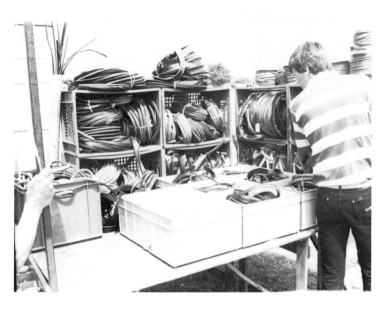

inside the car where the screwheads show, to finish them off by lining all the screwheads up. It was a nice little point always insisted upon in the service department of Rolls Royce where I worked in the mid 1950s.

A nicely refinished dash will make any worn or broken knobs, switches and similar bits and pieces stand out like a sore thumb. In most cases the best method is to replace them by hunting around at autojumbles or breakers' yards, but in some cases it is almost impossible to find the pieces you need because they will also have deteriorated on almost every car of that model. This particularly applies to the earlier type of plastic radio speaker grilles and some of the demisting vents which were made of a type of plastic which curled and buckled in the sunlight which beat down through the windscreen.

Quite good substitutes for these can be made from the type of moulding plastic which can be found in almost any craft shop and which is usually sold for embedding flowers, coins and similar small objects. You have to make a pattern first, and the best pattern of all is an original grille, so if this is warped, flatten it by making small cuts with a craft knife or small hack saw, tacking it down flat to a board and filling the cuts afterwards with almost any type of filler

An alternative to carpeting on the floor and seat back of an estate is aluminium rubbing strip. A cleaner for alloy wheels will brighten this, but it is advisable to take the strips off first, in case the chemical cleaner damages the rest of the trim. The same applies to aluminium kick-plates on door sills

such as Plastic Padding, David's Isopon or even with ordinary plaster of Paris.

To produce the new piece, make a female mould from the original; the rubber material for making the mould can be obtained from a craft shop. Usually this has to be heated to make it liquid, then poured over the pattern which has been painted or dusted with a releasing agent. Because the moulding material is rubber, it will deal with quite a few awkward shapes, but not with heavy re-entrant angles, so you may have to cut in with a craft knife or razor blade to get it off, and melt it down again afterwards to make a new mould if you need more than one of anything. If you have to cut the mould to get it off the original pattern, stick it together again with one of the Superglues, and any small flash line which is left afterwards on the reproduction moulding can be sandpapered down afterwards then polished out.

Techniques of making a mould vary, but the usual method with something flat like a speaker grille is to fasten it down to a board, paint the grille and the board with a releasing agent and then make a fence all the way round it. The moulding rubber is heated and poured in and, when it is set, eased out of the fence so that there is a rather floppy pattern with the shape of the grille pressed into it. To mould the new grille, put the rubber moulding down on a board and build another fence round it, mix the plastic and hardener and pour them in. You can buy colourings to mix in with the plastic resin before you add the hardener; most of these colours will intermix so that it is usually not too difficult to match the original colour of the moulding.

The mouldings you make in this way will be quite tough but fairly brittle where there are thin sections, so sometimes it is advisable to reinforce them with an interior wire. To do this pour in about half the plastic and let it set, just sufficiently for it to become hard enough to support the wire. Then lay the wire down in the mould and pour on the remaining plastic. Handles and knobs for switches can be made in the same way, but here you have the slight extra complication in that most of them are of such a shape that either the rubber mould must be made in two parts, or made it in one part and slit it down one side to get it off the original knob. Glue it together again with Superglue—a useful material which will stick most rubber mouldings, even sponge rubber, very securely—and when the new knob or handle is dry, cut the mould off again and clean up any flash lines. When you clean these flash lines off with very fine sandpaper, the surface of the plastic stays dull, but it can be brought up to a very high gloss quite easily with rubbing-down paste and metal polish.

Restoring instrument dials is usually best left to a professional with years of experience in fine sign writing, but if you want to have a go at it yourself, a wide variety of rub down lettering is available from most large stationers, from which you can choose alphabets and series of numbers to match the originals.

Chromium plated bezels to the instruments, or chromium plated levers and knobs which have worn, can easily be replated, provided they are not made of the soft aluminium and magnesium alloy which often develops pimples and other blemishes. Some platers will take these on, but others will say that it is impossible to replate them once they have started to corrode under the original plating. Even if you cannot find a part in better condition, and you can find a plater who will co-operate with you, it is still possible to make a very good job of renovating such parts.

Ask the plater to put them in his chemical cleaning tank, then return them to you before going any further. When you get them back, go over the blisters and pock marks with a small pointed tool, to dig out the dark pitted corrosion, and then fill the holes by rubbing with a piece of very soft copper. Any piece of copper can be made soft by heating it to a bright red and then plunging it into cold water—the same way as hardening a piece of steel, except that with copper this has the opposite effect. When all the pock marks have been filled with copper, return the pieces to the plater and ask him first to nickel plate and finally to finish off with chromium plating. He will probably charge you extra for this individual treatment, but if the parts are irreplaceable, it is worth the cost.

Steering wheels which have become badly rubbed or on which the plastic or celluloid covering has started to crack, always spoil the interior look of a car. Though there are specialist firms who will strip the old material off and recover the wheel for you, it is rather an expensive business. The easiest solution is to search around to find a secondhand replacement in much better condition. Small scratches and disfigurations can usually be polished out with rubbing down paste and metal polish, except on vinyl covered steering wheels where the only answer to wear and tear is to renew the covering.

Getting the steering wheel off can sometimes present a problem. On later cars it is usually fairly easy, because the centre medallion or finisher to the wheel *was* just a finisher, and when this is prised up with a small screwdriver, the fixing nut for the steering wheel can be seen immediately underneath. The older type of car is much more awkward and sometimes quite puzzling, where there were controls coming up through the centre of the steering column for the horn, trafficators and sometimes for the headlamp dip switch. In most cases the wiring was carried in a long steel tube which ran all the way down the length of the steering column and out through the bottom of the steering box. This was held at the bottom by a sleeve nut and a brass olive (to stop the oil running out of the box); when this nut and olive are removed the tube can be pulled up from the inside of the car. Be very careful how you lift out the tube from the inside, for it is quite long on some cars; if you bend it or kink it, it can be a dreadful job to get back in again.

Even with its fixing nut removed, the steering wheel can sometimes be quite a brute to shift, if it is held on tapered splines or on a tapered shaft with a key. Sometimes, gentle tapping on the underside of the boss—with a piece of wood as a buffer to stop bruising – will shift it, but in other cases you will have to use a steering wheel puller. These are very similar to a hub puller but have specially shaped jaws to fit underneath the boss of the steering wheel. It is not worth buying a puller just to get the steering wheel off once, so it is useful to speak nicely to your local garage and ask them either if you can borrow a puller against a deposit, or if they are unwilling to do this, if they will send a mechanic round with the puller to get the wheel off for you. In most cases I have found local garages very obliging for small jobs like this, because they often take an interest in the car you are restoring, particularly if it is one for which they hold the franchise, and it is good policy on their part to make a friend of you, so that they will then have a regular customer. Once you have befriended your local garage you will find that they can often produce bits and pieces, either from the back of their own stores, or by phoning round to other franchised garages. Very often there are old parts still held somewhere in the garage, which have not been required either for repair work or by customers for years. They are on the stock inventory somewhere, but the most reliable guide to where they are and what they are is the memory of the man on the parts counter, *if* you can get him interested in your restoration project.

But play fair with your garage. If they go to a lot of trouble to help you with obsolete parts, it is worth more than the few pennies lower price on more common items which you might find by shopping around, so patronize them as much as possible.

Index